# UNPAINTED PORTRAITS

PAUL ZEPPELIN

# UNPAINTED PORTRAITS

iUniverse books may be ordered through booksellers or by contacting:

iUniverse
1663 Liberty Drive
Bloomington, IN 47403
www.iuniverse.com
844-349-9409

Because of the dynamic nature of the Internet, any web addresses or
links contained in this book may have changed since publication and may
no longer be valid. The views expressed in this work are solely those
of the author and do not necessarily reflect the views of the publisher,
and the publisher hereby disclaims any responsibility for them.

Any people depicted in stock imagery provided by Getty Images are
models, and such images are being used for illustrative purposes only.
Certain stock imagery © Getty Images.

ISBN: 978-1-6632-3742-2 (sc)
ISBN: 978-1-6632-3741-5 (e)

Print information available on the last page.

iUniverse rev. date: 03/21/2022

# Contents

# Foreword

Paul Zeppelin is a poet with exceptional depth in his writing due to his vast experience and education.

His poetry often focuses on both the joy and pain of life and death; on loyalty and betrayal, on failures and successes, on broken hearts and sunlit hopes.

The poetry is full of, at times, a sarcastic wit, veiled humor, and intellectual clarity. It shows both deep insight and intriguing, controversial views of both individual and world issues.

Judith Parrish Broadbent

# Epigram

Teardrops don't heal our scars;
They never soothe our sorrows,
And yet, we write about delightful tomorrows
In our self-indulging, self-important memoirs.

# Portraits

The art of objectivity
Doesn't exist in portraits
Of my friends;
Even a doubtful resemblance
Has trace of my devotion
To the unhappy ends.

My modest talent flies
Between reality and dreams;
This thought-provoking journey
Tied the two with bumpy seams,
Then went to the far reaches
Of fading castles in the skies
And to the quivering yet horny,
Aggressively malicious threats
That mercilessly devour
My buddies disappearing portraits
And cynically leave a single flower.

## Forgotten Portraits

I am a steward of forgotten portraits
Almost erased by our merciless times,
Those faces look like spectral mimes
That shadowed their unhappy fates.

These precious family collections
Bring our own multiple reflections,
And yet remind me of a tattered floor
Where every scratch and stain
Recites its own praiseworthy story
And keeps the lifelong score
Until the final train
Delivers them to glory.

# Bordeaux

I didn't grow upside down;
No one has seen my roots.
I am not a red-nosed clown;
I never had to fill gigantic boots.

I only chat and travel,
I eat and drink
Until I hear the judge's gavel
Before I had a chance to blink.

These days, I travel through Bordeaux,
The land of Sauvignons and great Merlot,
The land of ancient chiseled poses
Of naked goddesses and gods,
The land of sparkling tiny roses
Surviving under the lightning rods
Of frequent summer thunderstorms;
Then, after the fertile ground warms
It shares nutritious juices with every vine
That is giving birth to a luscious wine,
The land of the most delicious meals
Expensive but within my credit line;
I feel as if I reached beyond the seven seals
And Bacchus shares with me his godly wine.

## But How

My poetry peels off the crafty nightly husk
And flaunts our globe from dawn to dusk.

The vast majority won't read the pages
With pompous images of our heroes,
We only see in the rearview mirrors
The images of trashy highway rages
And learn the flashy wartime lies
Instead of history of honorable lives...

I let unfairness of my rhymes
Be punishment without crimes,
I want my heartfelt verses
To flow like a urine of racehorses,
I want the penetrating grandeur of my lines
To be laconic as the street and traffic signs,
I carve my lyrics on the walls of public toilets
To please lieutenants, generals and privates,
To entertain my equals, the constipating vets.

I write about a spaceship or a prosaic plough
I trust, it doesn't matter what I write, but how.

## Luscious Feast

Oh, what a luscious feast for our hungry ears,
A happy laughter through pessimistic tears:

My boogie-woogie piano floats on "Swanee River",
Glenn Miller's band blows up "Saint Louis Blues",
A tiny Peggy Lee rejuvenates her famous "Fever",
While Elvis Presley walks his "Blue Suede Shoes",
Jerry Lee Lewis knocks away "Great Balls of Fire",
And Cohen urges "Dance Me to the End of Love".
My buddies say: "You are preaching to the choir",
Please, stop, enough is just enough.

I lived and truly loved that music and all the rest;
Perhaps in vain, I tried to do my very best,
Some say it was not very much,
But even that I can no longer reach and touch.

# Divinity of Grace

A tragic legacy of squeaky-clean beliefs
Placed us in the society of thieves
Wrapped in a quilt of so-called good desires
Completely useless like disconnected wires.

Is this the time to write a newer Bill of Rights,
Or reinterpret a much older Mathew's psalm
In my pursuit of lights and the divinity of calm
Beyond the never-ending hallowed fights?

Almighty dumped on us his keynote speech
About paradise no one will ever reach,
About our hopes that disappear at nights
And let nightmares devour our daily lights.
So many times I heard this speech before,
Faithfully repeated by my preacher,
By that well-known church's whore...

Isn't it a ripen time to change my teacher?

I am still searching for a quiet space
Without pious condescending speeches,
Where even my conscience wouldn't preach
Against a wonderful divinity of grace.

# I Waste the Ink

I write, I waste the ink but think
About powers of evenhanded tides
That lifted each and every boat;
Some of them later sink,
The others calmly float.

The law of life: survival of the fittest,
The gods are referees of this contest,
The sinless innocence of looming horses
Awaits hand coloring from the believers
Expecting the apocalyptic heavy hand.

It is the second coming of my verses,
It is the unrelenting flow of new rivers,
It is the beginning, not the end.

# Eternal City

So far away from home,
I am carrying my backpack,
I am once again in Rome,
A lure that brings me back.

I climb the Spanish stairs
I gaze at the cuddling pairs,
I chat to angels on the roofs,
I search the Vatican for truths,
I walk along the ruins of a Forum,
I analyze the arts of Sistine Chapel,
I hear the yelps of the Arena quorum,
I even see the carnal knowledge apple.

I love the Eternal City on seven hills,
I travel where my guiding angel wills.

# Bang

At times, we hear our inner voices
And veer between two only choices
Get sucked into a devouring black hole
Or marvel at the gods' amazing power
Each year and month, each day and hour;
There is no simple way to understand
The rules of our enigmatic universe:
Did someone play a crucial role
And whisper the unknown word
Or write for us the primal epic verse
And disconnect the amniotic cord?

It seems that so-called cultured people
Accept the common scientific slang:
Live long and welcome the Big Bang.

# Portofino

We are again in Portofino,
Our late dinner quietly begun,
A waiter poured a tasty Pinot
And our anxiety has gone.

Two candles tremble in her eyes;
Is it a sign of a farewell?
Is there a secret she won't tell?
Or will we be together till sunrise?

Will she return to him?
Will I return to her?
Is this the end of our whim?

A stolen glee is never duty-free.
Even the Lord may not deter
The sins of lust and love…
For me it's good enough.

# My World

My heart is trembling
Just like a banner on a mast
My boat is still remembering
My marriages that didn't last

I am as guilty as a mortal sin,
I choke and drown in my love affairs,
Hot as a cup of coffee in a drive-in,
Unstable as the broken chairs.

My genuine confessions never help,
Whether I am mute or yelp;
A typical catch twenty-two:
No one believed them on my street,
Or laughed at me on every avenue.

Life's going on,
I am not waiting for a singing swan;
I siphoned my sixth Maker's Mark,
And sunk into my cozy world.
Each barfly acted like a happy lark,
My banner was fearlessly unfurled.

## Seven Wins

In my lifelong lineup
I see a few significant milestones:
The day of my unexpected birth,
The drinking of a sacramental cup,
The pompous burial of my soulless bones.

I no longer dwell on Earth
But left my seven books behind,
My seven mortal sins
My only seven wins
That will enrich the open mind.

# Escape

The future dumps on us
Some insincere linguistic acrobatics,
We are confused; we fall under the bus,
And lose our physics and mathematics;
We lose our treasures to the scam,
We choose to sacrifice another lamb.

Even a genius idea dies in the dark
If no one starts a bonfire from that spark.
We navigate the ship of fools
But never dock at colleges and schools.

We watch our tomorrows
Which are taking shape
With their own highs and lows
But we are hiding on the fire escape.

# The Dial

My final hour is flashing on the dial,
My pills are looming on the table,
I am chugging along my extra mile,
And grow wings to fly above a gable.

I am not waiting for the parting call,
And I do not want to jump the queue
To meet St. Peter and St. Paul;
I want to see the diamonds of morning dew.

I lost my trust in heavens,
There are no pies or watermelons
For my eternal dinner
Whether I am a winner or a sinner;
I definitely am none of the above,
I am a simple man who hates to hate
But loves to love.

# The Perfect Human God

The making of archaic mavens,
Who used to be above the fray,
He is art in bliss or heavens,
Luring the hordes of people
That faithfully sing and pray
Under the church's steeple.

Each of our dear lives
Comes with
A certificate of death,
We trudge
Through our strifes
Until the final breath.

We're trusting naked trees
Within intolerance of creeds.
We try to change the cores
Of grisly wars without peace,
Unfortunately, our noble deeds
Can't end disastrous encores.

From the fields and riverbanks
Of every biblical temptation,
We're climbing the shiny ranks
Towards our great creation,
Towards the lightning rod,
Towards the perfect human god.

# Alzheimer

I keep forgetting everything:
The trivia that has to be dismembered,
And things that have to be remembered,
And even the basic three plus seven
Ignited my frustration;
I need to find a safe haven
For what is left of my imagination.

Life is unfair; it must be told,
Some dare to zig, some dare to zag,
Some dig the shiny gold,
The others get a bag to hold;
While in the bar, watch what is brewing,
Do not compete with barflies, dude
The fat you are still chewing
They have already chewed.
I managed to forget these codes,
Today, I walk the other roads.

No big ideas, just tiny morsels,
I know less than I knew before,
I can no longer read the labels,
My memories are like horses
That left the stables;
I just forgot to lock the door.
I put my blazer in a microwave
And turned the timer,
Another triumph of Alzheimer!

# Thoughtless Gift

My longest journey
Into the secrets of eternal life
Has started from a tricky serpent
And his miraculously honeyed fruit:
From being naked, hungry, free and horny,
From knowing love without jealousy and strife,
From living in the Eden garden without paying rent,
From the first human race wearing only a birthday suit.

There is a minor rift
Between myself and our Lord,
It is a thoughtless gift
Of never-ending procreation:
While our planet is revolving,
While we are still evolving
From the Big Bang or the word
Into a vague civilization yet unknown,
I am afraid that our great nation
May crash the cornerstone,
The constitution; the foundation.

## Unknown End

I keep my friendships with Makers Mark
And scrumptious Chateau Neuf du Pape,
Thereby, I crawl under the rainbow arc
To get into my favorite pawnshop.

There are no golden nuggets in the weeds,
I searched but couldn't see a single ounce;
My banker said: "Dead cats don't bounce,
There is no value in your current deeds".

I act as if I am destined to upend
Our contaminated paradigm,
As if I want to cease the trend
That lets our blind justice turn on a dime
And justify the means by the unknown end.

I don't remember what I have known,
A left my soul and intellect ajar,
My secrets were immediately blown,
Alzheimer is already playing my guitar:
The memory is fading; it is my time to go,
The boneyard looms just a stone throw...

## Darker End

My train's excessive confidence
Leads to a careless attitude
Toward essential details;
And only my angelic providence
Keeps me away from a fatal feud
Between two shiny iron rails,
Between their feigned smiles
Devouring the never-ending miles.

My fated terminal remains evasive,
I guess, the saints don't want me in,
The darker end appears pervasive;
I will be surprised if I will ever win...

# Maturity Arrived

Last night, so-called maturity arrived;
Sex breathed but was deprived,
Then greed became a sparkling star
And a dominating force;
I had to change my course
And ran the luscious streams of joy
Between the chapters of my ploy.

Sex, love and greed,
Three major forces of a life, indeed,
Until a parting breath,
Until we are overwhelmed by death.
Some people trust in bliss,
Some others in the abyss:
Eternal hell or heaven for the crowds
And the infinity of void for our doubts.

I know seven reasons
To enjoy the seven mortal sins
Under the seven arches of a rainbow,
Under that colorful godsend mystique.
But cannot find just a single reason
After my rare defeats and a few wins
To turn my other cheek.

I am independent in my glee,
Fait accompli.

# Sisyphean Boulders

I reached the sky from wide Sisyphean shoulders
And watched the ups and downs of his boulders.

The sun lit clouds with my dreams,
While I weaved verses from the sunny beams;
I used nearly each word from my workbox,
But couldn't save the chickens,
The guiding angels hired me to feed the fox.
I am still knitting yet my better rhyme
And waiting in the line to get cheap tickets
Into the promised land of heaven's paradigm.

Am I a snake that can no longer rattle?
Am I just a showboat; big hat, no cattle?

# Peace Died

They wrote about business lunches
And the most exquisite dinners,
About the the abstinent and boozers...
The histories were written by the winners,
Rewritten later by the losers,
And edited much later piece by piece
By those who never fought in wars
But never treasured peace.

Slightly ahead of my own skis
I watched tomorrows in the hourglass
And saw the ornamented military brass
Shed their epaulettes and medals
Just like the autumn flowers and trees
Get rid of their golden leaves and petals.

I marched and yelped "Make love, not war!"
But was awakened by the noises outdoor,
It was a pompous funeral procession's ride,
Peace died.

# Nobody Reads

My poetry is a confession,
It is not a bald-faced propaganda,
It bares my mind and soul,
It is my conscience' gentle toll.
It is a meekly waged profession,
It is a voyage of my rights and wrongs,
It is a merciless hit-and-run commando
That lets me sing my own songs;
It is a singling out, mocking wraith,
It is a graveyard of my fragile faith.

I write, I sow some fertile seeds,
Nobody reaps, nobody reads.

# Band of Sinners

Our hunger doesn't invite us to a table,
Great cooking, luscious wines
And clever people do;
Their enigmatic stories and witty fables
Are stronger magnets and a tougher glue
That binds us all together;
We are those soul-birds of a feather
That flock to the most lavish dinners.
We are the marching band of sinners.

# My Own Ride

I rinsed the ballroom of my youth,
No shadows on the walls,
No scratches on the floor,
The drapes are pulled aside,
No radios, no phones, no calls,
The widows opened wide.

The naked showered truth,
My future sprawls before the door,
I left my yesterdays, at last;
I am a kid who doesn't need a guide
To break through ancient overcast
And start my own one-way ride.

# Luck

My heart runs like a buffalo to a waterhole,
I am playing poker in Las Vegas,
The towers of chips run out of control
And drown in the soup of alphas and omegas.
I hid my nerves and calmly bluffed,
In poker it is not a crime, I won't be cuffed,
I am a lucky pokerfaced beginner,
My stare was absolutely blank,
Until I was declared a winner...

I am still whistling Dixie past my bank.

# Tin Angels

Tin angels turn above the gables
To see the baby-bringing storks,
Those babies grow up wrapped
In their parents' cozy fables;
Only tin angels sieve the witty from
The goofy dorks,
But keep their secrets under
The seven seals.
We play our modest hands,
The gods reject our appeals.

My eyes reflect a morbid fascination
With the ethereal stardust,
I am the face of a shiny culmination
Of a mind-numbing lust.

I strolled along my destiny and fate,
And learned from angels to separate
The forests from the trees,
A tempest from a morning breeze.

Even a double helix of my DNA
Will not reveal my core,
I am not all-you-can- eat-buffet,
I dare to play; some others only
Keep the score.

# Fountain of Youth

Discovery of carnal knowledge
And a captivating joy of puppy love
Entered my energetic youth
Sometime in the beginning of my teens.
It is a devastating truth,
But so-called deep and real love
I knew much later in a college…
Please, don't let me spill the beans,
The ends will always justify the means.
And yet, here is the truth:
I miss that tender puppy love,
I miss the real Fountain of Youth.

# Ponte Saint Angelo

Alone in Rome;
Ploughing my way
Along the sidewalk sales,
Two handsome marble angels
Guide me to St. Peter's Dome,
Although I am too old to pray,
I slowly walk and hold the rails,
I need to cross the Angelo Bridge.

St. Michael waves a sword,
St. Gabe plays a golden horn;
But I already heard the word,
But I already tried to be reborn,
And yet, I see the sun above the ridge.

# Until a Fat Swan Sings

I outlived my friends,
I outlived my foes,
I outlived my joys and my despairs;
Without pride there are no happy ends,
Death easy comes,
Life easy goes,
Without vanity there are no love affairs.

I hid my bag of wasted wedding rings
And tuned myself into the new adventures,
But my sub-conscience said:
"You have to grow just a pair of wings,
Then learn to fly and imitate an angel
Until a fat swan sings…
And don't forget to clean your dentures,
To chew a gum and to refresh your breath
Before you start to date a total stranger;
Besides, keep in your mind,
Excessive sex may lead to death."

I answered: "Never mind."
And like that famous weepy Hamlet
I presumed: "To be or not to be,
If she will die, she dies,
You will see my teary eyes,
So let it be; the end of glee,
The end of yet another pamphlet."

# Silver Spoon

I meet my buddies in the bar,
Some are subdued, the others star;
Life tastes and pulls us in and out,
Life is a hungry hound and a scout.

I didn't trash my well-developed mind,
My buddies always ask for my advices,
They eagerly demanded, I supplied:
They learned the values and the prices.

My better foot was not put forward,
I woke in peace but ended up in war,
I only had slim chances in the world
To live and cast a shadow on the floor.

Our galaxy is quite a lovely place,
And that is why I turned about-face
And landed on the moon
I am in the pursuit
Of my once stolen birthright's silver spoon,
Deceptively a low-hanging fruit.

# Trashcan Alleys

Why do I do so much
Against my wishes?
I never understood my role as such
Among the broken hearts
And empty broken dishes
While dodging the cupid's darts.

At times, I muddle through
My narcissistic personality,
Here is a clue for you,
I reassessed the intricate reality
And realized that I am rife
With talents and desires;
I satisfy my ego only
But not the morbid curiosity
Of my empty-bellied mind and eyes.

The blue attracts my eyes,
The black attracts my mind,
The bas-relief of hills and valleys
Attracts my fragile skinless soul.
At night I am dreamy and refined:
I see the castles in the skies,
But walk the trashcan alleys
And disappear in that black hole.

# Sipping

My memory contains confessions and remorses,
Most come from the time of service in the forces;
I used to kill my enemies in so-called self-defense,
I used to shoot whatever moved beyond the fence.

Today, I am trolled by my beloved brandy
Into the ruthless images of red sunsets,
Using my drinking modus operendi
To justify my wartime deep regrets.

I bask in every sunny day,
At night, I stand atop of a flight of stars
And lick my wounds and scars
In the pursuit of my own, more gentle way.

A wick is playing with the flame,
The wax is slowly dripping,
I closely watch this naughty game,
Cuddling a brandy glass and sipping.

# Seagulls

I am a total wreck:
Ferocious schedule of my flights
Across the better world,
Don't let me see the lights.
Just take my word,
I have no aces in my basic deck.

I am already on my way,
I daily bite the bait,
I trust in fate and DNA,
A problem? Let's debate.

The time forever lulls
The headwinds of reality,
Only the brave and proud seagulls
Hover above the raging seas,
And Neptune sets them free
Into the ever-present breeze.

Tomorrows are reflected
In my empty plate,
No pulse detected,
It is too late.

# Drinking Habits

I didn't watch sunrises,
I only watched sunsets,
I noticed grass still rises,
The gamblers place their bets.

My doctor asked
To change my drinking habits,
I have avoided drinking
For the past five years,
I made my life so grim,
Don't ask me why; I trusted him.
It was a showbiz, I wasn't thinking,
I ran from the self-inflicted fears;
I wore a hat without hidden rabbits.

# Constant Vortex

Life was a virgin when we accidentally met,
Tall and white-skinned like a Russian birch;
We traveled, ate and drank, we loved, and yet,
Sometimes, she acted like a whore in church.

But we are together and in love. I am still alive.
All our exiting feats move in a constant vortex,
Just like my conscience in the cerebral cortex.
I married life. Until my final breath life is my wife.

# Elysian Fields

I am in the pursuit of paradise
I roam the false Elysian Fields,
I search; I am all ears and eyes,
But see the STOPs and YIELDs.

I need two answers to memorize
When I am finally up there:
"What was the asking price?
Was it too high or fair?"

Life is a mysterious cliffhanger,
I am alive, it takes some time,
I am not a goose, I am a gander,
Don't write me off, I am in my prime:
I want to be both strong and tender,
I even let my sleepy wisdom climb.

I'd rather take a second chance
To leave the first impression..
I'd rather be present but divided
Between a bright exuberance
And a low-spirited depression.
I'd rather ride
My thoroughbred superiority
Than settle in a pigsty
Of a dead-end inferiority.

I mastered a sophisticated art
Of keeping my personalities apart
Without any therapies and drugs,
Just the New Year's kisses,
And the Easter's hugs.

# Perhaps

I've got the wrong end of the stick
When we first met,
I was too gullible, she was too slick.
I was red-haired, she was a beautiful brunette.

I knew a bit about foreign rules and manners
And called to mind our own crests and banners.
This happened in Madrid, on Spanish land
And went so well as if it was somehow planned.

She shared with me her extra ticket
To a gold-speckled concert hall;
The music was intriguing, captivating, wicked,
It touched my withered thirsty soul,
It woke me up, thrilled and renew,
As if I climbed the tallest wall
And saw ahead of me much brighter avenue.

The night collapsed.
We loved.
Dawn has arrived on time.
Perhaps,
Tomorrow, I'll carve a better rhyme.

# Dull Crossbones

Ideas aren't good enough
If they are poorly worded.
Even my gentle love
Gets sick and tired
If it is not rewarded.

I live among the angry roosters
In the bloody cockpit of this life,
I even ace the greedy boosters
Fueling my never-ending strife.

I haven't learned to hide my greed,
My deep desires and raw emotions,
While I am sailing seas and oceans,
The boneyards of the pirates' ships
With gold, not with the riskers' chips.

I haven't learned to walk the waters,
I have no use for dimes and quarters
Dumped in the shallow Sea of Galilee,
I am longing to unearth the real glee,
The diamonds, sapphires and other stones
Instead of jaded skulls and dull crossbones.

I want to meet the mermaids and leviathans
Besides the other underwater monsters,
I am fed-up with halibuts and lobsters;
I haven't learned to hide my greed,
I listen to my inner wicked voice:
Success in guaranteed.

## Truisms

Only a genius can be transfixed
By the unsayable that may exist.
A man won't stumble lying in his bed,
Lethargy is valued only by the dead.
If you are a friend with everyone,
You have a real friendship with no one.
Even in a total garbage gold is not brass,
Those who are left behind will bite your ass,
Grapes never need a prayer, just some rain,
There is no free lunch, no gain without pain.

# Good Enough

I looked-for a trusted brother,
But got completely lost
Between the Father,
Jesus and the Holy Ghost...

I was a dog teased with a bone,
I was a coalmine sacrificial canary,
I was a dice that has been thrown
But fell into a someone's bloody Mary.

I never knew the girl I loved,
I was entirely blinded by her beauty.
She was an iron hand so tightly gloved
As if she was a cruel prison guard on duty.

I haven't gotten a much better lover,
But lived and let myself discover
How to dance her to the end of love;
I think, for me it's good enough.

# Decaffeinated Mind

I wrapped too many dreams in my tortillas,
The welcoming tequilas swallowed my ideas.

Am I still living on a borrowed time?
Who is that charitable lender?
Will he accept from me a silver dime
For my unearned unending splendor?

Do I still battle windmills
In my decaffeinated mind?
Do I rewrite the foolish wills
And leave those fates behind?

I wish a had a plentiful infusion of common sense
When I was hiking through the labyrinths of youth;
The grass was greener beyond the shallow fence,
But every lie looked like a clean-cut truth.

Someone pulled a great idea from the net:
"Life is a box of chocolate,
You never know what you get,
But very few remember this as yet."

# Healing Balm

We lived defined by isolation
Under a constant threat
Of missing once-in-a life elation.

St. Michael blew his horn
To state his principal intention
And crashed the bone of our contention.
The truth was born.

We wastefully rested on our laurels
And flaunted our old ill-fated morals.

I slashed my palm
To check
If I still feel.
You used to be my healing balm,
I used to be a man of steel;
These days, I am a wreck.
We both have tickets for the trip,
Let's make a deal:
I am not a sinking ship,
And you are not an upper deck.

# Less Amused

I firmly trust in innocence of prostitution,
There is no end to my heartfelt despair,
Only a vicious prosecution of innocence
Deserves a merciless lifetime sentence,
An everlasting dreadful nightmare...

No one can be less critical more often,
No one can be more often less amused
Then us when we escort our own coffin
And see a made-up face we never used.

Even a silver coin has two sides,
We wear the masks on our faces
To be in every battle of the minds
And disappear without traces.

I lined my foes and friends
In order of their apparent non-importance,
Even the longest threads have ends...
The end of one is the beginning of another.
They stretch like harmless garden serpents
To recognize each other in their brother.

The Wisdom Tree
Still casts its shadow in the Eden garden.
Even the most unblemished glee
Commits the sins that need a pardon.

I try to meander on a higher path,
But feel the heavy hand of wrath.

# Lifelong Marathon

I have to struggle if I must
Through pointless twilights of a reason,
Through no-way-out swamps of treason,
To see ascensions of loyalty and trust.

I stirred my flattened wishes,
Unfurled my restless sails,
And honed my craving arrows.
My future promised to remain delicious,
My nowadays explained the fairytales,
Meanwhile, my focus sharply narrows:
My life is not a dreary marathon,
It is a lightning strike of sprint,
It is my time to read the smallest print.

I am alone, without foes and friends,
My lifelong odyssey abruptly ends.
I am blinded by the outburst of light,
But see the fiery bush
And hear the roaring voice:
"Here are the Ten Commandments
For you to mourn or to rejoice!"

# Single Candle

It was a lovely picnic
Only a single candle
Burned on my birthday cake
And skillfully masked my age.

I didn't want a birthday scandal,
I made a wish and I blew the wick,
It was that never-going-out fake,
I hid in blissful smiles my outrage.

I was surrounded by younger folks
Not bothered with the nasty strokes.

Here is some trivia I picked, at last:
To know real face of happiness,
One had to be ill-fated in the past
And know both, delight and stress.

No one grows older
At the dining table,
We drink a lot of wine
And get much bolder;
My horse is waiting
Saddled in his stable,
But I am not ready
To cross the final line.

# That Switch

Life was a somewhat bitch,
The switch was within reach,
Gas leaked, I didn't turn it off,
Then stuck my head into a stove,
But quickly changed my morbid mind,
Somebody bit, excuse me, my behind,
I pulled my head, it was my French bulldog.

I didn't start to write my epilogue,
I am still walking through the weeds
In search of cultured and well-read.
At least, I write, therefore I am not dead,
And often dream of better times and deeds.

I am entertained by the falling golden leaves,
I am entertained by the climbing blinding sun,
I am entertained by the imaginative thieves
And keep unloaded my ancient shotgun.

It is so nice to be a charmed bystander,
Because what is quite good for a dull goose,
Sometime is not that good for a smart gander.
As I already said, life is unfair and quite a bitch,
I beg you, please, don't ever turn that switch.

# Daily Lathe

Life is a waiting room
Filled with impatient patients
That hampered with their chains
Some take the pill to kill their gloom,
Some just surrendered to their chronic pains,
The others were the trains that left the stations.

A preacher came with bells and whistles
To lure me into his bewildered faith,
I use my palette knives and bristles,
I am revolving in a-no-way-out daily lathe
Of my deceitfully painted heartless world.

I shredded the umbilical and every other cord.

I veer between hope, love and hate
Life is the game of cat-and-mouse,
I spin like waltzes of Johann Strauss,
I aim and faithfully negotiate,
I pay attention to each detail,
Nevertheless, I bit the bait,
I promised not to sin but failed;
Even the vowed daily bread
My angels previously ate.

My misconceptions are forever gone,
The fallen angels have been outdone.

# Cunning Words

A sunset paints the heavens purple
Despite the tears of artsy mourners,
Even a square may turn into a circle
If I will stretch its perky corners.

The ancient Romans used to say:
"At night all cats look gray,
At night a predator becomes a prey;
Even a flower may provide a lethal bite
In hope that no one sees it from the sky
Or they can't separate a poison and a pie."

The gods must know all these things,
The saints won't notice or remember,
The angels fail to protect and guide;
Therefore, some get a pair of lucky wings,
Majority enjoys a life adamant yet tender,
The others still don't know they have died.

I used to understand the genuine truth,
I saw that facts were naked as the birds
And pure as the innocence of our youth,
It was before I learned the cunning words.

# Barflies

A happy hour begins at five,
Only the dead cats never bounce,
But as one can see I am still alive;
Pour in my glass at least an ounce
Of your best Armagnac to taste,
If I won't like, I'd never waste.

It is the start of my weekend,
The owner argues with the band,
They ask more money for the night,
It is without doubt quite exciting, right?

I chewed the fat with everyone around
And offered them on-me this round;
I love these lonesome veteran barflies,
They often cross my t's and dot my i's.
They see no news under the risen sun,
Their thrilling happy days have gone.

I wonder whether I live in this despair,
I truly wish and hope
Life will surprise me with a worthy flair
Or I will need a sturdy rope.

I see my face in a half-empty glass
And my thumbprints on its shiny walls,
I think it is my wine of a Sunday mass
And hope my guiding angel never falls.

# Politicians

Our corrupted politicians
The real prison guards,
The common outlaws
But with the keys
Who guard our darkness
Wrapped in a heavy breathing
And accidental yelps or moans.
They are pitiless and heartless
But we are infants before teething,
Who gave them our flesh and bones

I checked my buddies' pockets:
Some flaunt their gold and silver,
Some hide their brass and copper;
Here is the real showstopper:
We win or lose the lifetime race,
Some grab the horn of plenty,
Some hold the empty buckets,
Some try to catch a falling knife,
Some fly into the space
In their own rockets.

I let myself play devil's advocate,
I passed the colorful yard signs,
Then crossed the party lines,
And chose the opposition candidate.

# Sommelier

I have a life, I am not ill, I need no cure,
I am a gorger and gourmand,
I am a master sommelier and epicure,
I am loaded with the greatest wines,
I catch the tickets then pay the fines,
And fall into the arms a pretty blonde.

It sounds like the ancient cliché:
I love La Tache, Richbourg and Romanee-conti,
I love Grand Echezeaux and Le Montrachet,
I love Lafite Rothschild, Louis La Tour and Haut Brion,
I love Chateau Margot and Chateau Petrus,
And by-the-way, I learned to cook from Paul Bocuse
In the Burgundian great city of Lyon.

For mediocre meals and wines I have no use.

We cheerfully click our Redel wineglasses
Like boxers knock their gloves before a fight,
We sip our wine like nectar for the masses,
It is our sacramental and inherited birthright.

# Wisdom Tree

My conscience is nearly gone,
I trust no one, besides my gun,
It may be a horrid thing to say.
I am an actor. Life is my stage,
My fate composed this script,
My wings are forever clipped,
I simply read the lines and play,
Only close friends are outraged.

My brain is like a tinderbox,
A single spark may blow it up,
Just pour me a Bloody Mary
Or the espresso coffee cup,
And I will be crazy like a fox.

I live in a psychedelic glee,
I earned it from the gods,
They gave me better odds,
I reached the Wisdom tree.

# Change

The birds are sitting on the wires,
They look like the music notes
So very few can play,
Only the churches' choirs
Can sing those tunes and pray.

The Bill of Rights insists,
Please, hold your horses.
Try to be better, change,
Says what we call the Book.

I know what is valuable,
I am a moneychanger,
I serve the gullible,
Am I a crook?

The mavens used to say,
Life is a well-written play,
Except for the final act:
Get ready to be sacked.

I tried to edit pages of my life,
But couldn't change a word;
Is it a praiseworthy strife?
Is there a glory or a reward?

# Debutante Ball

It is a mouth-watering performance
Of a white-gowned perky debutante,
A father-daughter yet informal dance,
It is a night life gifts you as a chance
To be introduced to a "polite" society
The symbol of out-of-date propriety.

A futile institution of the dying world,
An appetizer for a yet unknown dinner,
It is a wobbly echo of the primal word
Which must create a loser or a winner.

Some uncontrolled smirks and smiles
Are tightly glued to gorgeous faces
Expecting thousands of heavy miles
Of never-ending and competing races.

Sometimes, a life is turning
Into a hard-hitting hockey puck,
I wish them a great journey
And good luck!

# Camouflaged

I still remember the lullaby
My nanna sang for me,
So many moons passed by,
Unchained and set me free
From gullibly syrupy nights,
From an unending carnival of lights
Predicted by my beloved granny,
So sunny and angelically uncanny:
"Don't let them hold you down,
Each time we act, we lose or gain,
We all can rule or reign,
But only one will wear the crown."

I stoically survived
The labyrinths of life,
Where hatred and deceit
Are camouflaged but rife.

# Lackluster Alley

My preordained croupier announced:
"This game is over; no more bets."
The ball rolled up and bounced...
Today, I am learning to enjoy sunsets.

Each morning after sleepless nights,
I say, long live casino's luring lights,
And watch the river and its floating sun
Through my half opened sunken eyes,
I watch a cheering welcomed dawn,
I watch the triumph of sunrise.

Those gambling nights
Slowly descending to the gloomy end:
No more green tables
Under the blinding lights,
No more exaggerated winning fables
And money doesn't stream like sand
Between my trembling fingers,
Although, my dreary life still lingers.

My glee was canceled like a TV play
Without a striking, meaningful finale,
Life morphed into a lackluster alley,
I stroll alone on feet of clay...

## Daily Bread

I hear my lawyer's roar
And retaliate in-kind,
The goddess-justice is not blind,
She is a greedy whore;
When money starts to talk,
Her shaky fairness takes a walk.

I can't exhale the bitter smoke
Of my dire past,
So many wounds don't ever heal,
They failed to toss the heavy yoke,
Sweet memories don't ever last
Even with my nerves of steel.

God only gifts a day,
I earn my daily bread and meal.

# Rocking Cars

Goodbye maternity;
Our dreams created
Elegantly seductive pictures
Of a thought-provoking world
Along the boundless eternity
Which outlived the other fixtures
That severed Mother Nature's cord
In our pursuit of the elusive Lord.

I didn't drown in quagmires,
God passed by me that bitter cup,
Instead, he sent the Holy Ghost
To drive my Winnebago,
And fortunately its squeaky tires
Decided to abruptly wake me up
Right in the center of my town-host
The sunny, friendly San-Diego.

A bubbly life was screaming
In restaurants and bars,
A fiery love was steaming
On backseats of the rocking cars.

The fallen angel slammed the gavel:
Eat, drink, chat, make love and travel.

Whether or not
Sisyphus rolls his boulder,
Whether or not
The sun still hangs above my gable,
No one ever gets older
At the dining table.

# Squanderer

It is much easier to teach a horse to sing
Than to dress up a naked marching king;
Even a murderer won't kill in self-defense,
Nor I am a squanderer of common sense.

I see why people never learn their history
From books snoring on the grubby shelves;
They are too dull despite a dark mystery
That lets my conscience introduce myself.

Life is the theater of the absurd,
I went to war against my own time,
I was among the chosen few who heard
The clock of Judgment Day began to chime.

# Numb

I often lose my way
And get into the weeds,
Nobody lives a better day
Among the threaded beads.

No losses have a pleasing scent
When they are hiding on a shelf.

Today, I feel emotionally numb,
My short relationships are vacant,
The lifelong struggle with myself
Has ended in a draw for both,
Each was reluctant to succumb
And exercise our undying loath.

I couldn't lose what I didn't own,
I simply learned to stroll alone.

# Rerun

I am flying to the West,
Away from the rising sun,
I am a self-invited guest
Of those who stay alive,
Who breathe and thrive;
I need just one more day
To see the dawn's rerun,
To see a gentle sunny ray,
Just one more precious time
Before I carve my final rhyme.

I trust my intuition,
My final hours are near,
My angel acts like a mortician,
A wingless bastard, but so dear.

# Gift

I've got a never-wanted gift
From my renowned predecessors:
Bad knees, cholesterol and gout,
Besides an arm I can no longer lift.
A bunch of them were doctors and professors,
As a result, my IQ is exceptionally high
And everybody knows why
I often bend to pick my nickels
In front of a fast steamroller;
I am autistic and dangerously polar...

I buy Ferraris and trade them for tricycles.

## My Verse

I am supposed to stay in line and wait
Until the pencil-pushers read my verse
And write their pontificating disapproval
As a request for my permanent removal.

It is a common game of love-and-hate
Among the critics and literary whores.
But I am not a whore as such,
I wrote and read my verse
And liked it very much.

# Pain

You stole my heart,
My trust and my belief;
It was your trade, your art,
I was a fool, you were a thief.

The all-consuming rain
Erased even a trace of love;
You didn't feel my pain,
A predator can't be a dove.

# Eclipse

The sun was fading
I moved into the spotlight
Before the sharks arrived
Sent by the fiery raging night
Of the dog-tired ancient abyss,
Both evil and good were trading,
Ignoring the ill-fated boring bliss.

I am not sure that gentle dawn survived
To face the power of colorful Apocalypse,
To face the promised four-horses ride,
To face the merciless once-in-a-life eclipse.

# Whiskey Stream

The night sends every dying star
To drown in my granny's pond...

I am already a much bigger fish,
I need a lavish over-the-top dish,
I need the never-ending oceans,
While I am squandered in the bar
In the arms of a most striking blond
And wipe the tears of my emotions,
The tears of happiness without pain
Like sunny skies after a hurricane.

I am like a wind-filled sail
Rushing across the endless blue
In the pursuit of the Holy Grail;
I am in the pursuit of only you.

We never met;
You walk along my sacred dream
As a magnificent blue-eyed brunette,
As a heartwarming ray of light;
I couldn't stop my whiskey stream
And gently disappeared into the night.

# Vivre

A tough and unforgiving life runs
By fathers, widowers and sons,
Who mourn demises of the bravest ones,
By mothers, widows and their daughters,
The other victims of endless slaughters,
Collecting pensions' dimes and quarters.

Our vicious planet is not a sanatorium
That cures our chronic ailments and bashes;
Our globe is an effective crematorium
That burns our flesh and bones to ashes.

I used to live on this vindictive planet,
I've never been a miserable griever,
Even my tomb alleges on its granite:
Here rests in peace
A guarding angel of le art de vivre.

## Delicious Fruit

My garden happily awakened
From the eternity of a winter slumber,
The sun, an offhand cook is something baking,
I am not keen to taste, I am not a gambler.

The wisdom-tree is brightly blooming,
The first confusions and mistakes are looming:
The first two humans were asked to procreate:
Eve grabbed the most delicious fruit and ate;
Then why Adam and Eve were cruelly expelled?
Through centuries the verdict was upheld.

This was just at the beginning of the world.
Oh, what a mess. Just take MY word.

# Yet Unsigned

I dragged my tired feet
Like a scarred fighter in defeat
And only my impatient mind
Recited my death verdict yet unsigned
By the corrupted judge,
Who didn't care to hide his grudge;
Even the brick-faced jury hid their fury.
I saw their angry and bloodthirsty eyes,
If I were a devil, I'd rather wear a disguise.

A golden trembling image
Stubbornly lingers in my mind;
It is my almost forgotten village
Where I was born but left behind.

The shady past declares its death,
The future celebrates its birth,
The night parts with its breath,
A new day dawns above earth.
Is this a long-awaited paradigm,
Or evil is just turning on the dime?

The horses run behind their carts,
The cupids aim but miss our hearts.
Long live our distressing times,
Our harsh punishments, without crimes.

# Daring Horses

A little down from the north,
A little farther from the sun,
I am moving back and forth
Or simply walk or even run.

I cry when I see meat-wagons
Carrying some quiet corpses;
The wildest and daring horses
That didn't know dos and don'ts
They left this all-consuming life
Defeated in a merciless strife.

I envy those ten-headed dragons
Or a few brainless pumpkins less,
Who live their never-ending lives
And just for fun kidnap a princess.

But for a young girl's sake
There is a great warrior St. George
The fearless dragon-slayer,
And nothing helps that giant-snake,
Even the most wholehearted prayer.

# Weaving Street

I am not an iceberg,
You see the most of me,
You see my streets and avenues,
You even see my secrets in the news.

You see my ebbs and flows,
You see my rivers and rainbows,
You see my arteries and veins,
You see my losses and my gains.

I do what I was born to do,
I breathe, I have a life,
I may lose a battle or a useless strife,
At times, I even catch a falling knife...

Even if a half of what I wrote is true,
It is enough for anyone to amble through.
Life is a bus on a one-way weaving street,
Say grace and take a comfy seat.

# No More Bets

The night is perfect for romancing,
The quartet effortlessly playing,
I guess somebody is still playing,
And we are slowly dancing.

A humble choir of pain
Sounds like a growing grass,
A little creek veers into a drain
Hidden under the autumn brass.

Time melted in the hit of afternoon,
It is a suicide committed by the sun,
Almost almighty but not immune
To days of reckoning that just begun.

And then I hear:
It's over, no more bets,
Too late.
The flairs of sunsets
Vanishing but whisper,
Wait,
The sun will reappear.

# Underground

I went to see my buddy's corpse,
We fought together in a war;
I saw his runny nose,
I saw his moving toes.
Was he a born-again believer?
Was he a religious deceiver?

I take my days and nights
Straight at face value,
I often cast the dice
To learn the real price,
To see a clearer view,
To see the lights...

Nobody sees the flipside of my face:
The grimaces of pain,
The teardrops of despair,
The foggy trace
Of happiness that disappears,
The heartless verdict of my peers,
The broken life that is beyond repair.

The rules are bent,
The sun went underground,
We are hell-bound.

# Judge

Don't ever judge,
You won't be judged...
It's one of those malicious
Chocking lies
Of leaders who've been elected
And self-appointed preachers.

My conscience, soul and mind
Were appalled, which was expected,
My Sunday school obedience is behind:
I am a poet, I am self-elected,
I am a judge of cunning teachers,
I am a judge of lying powerholders,
I am a judge of hidden nonbelievers,
Of real devil-worshipers, our preachers.

I couldn't hear it from a silent mime:
But there is no AM; it is a coffee time,
And there is no PM; it is a whisky time.

## Confused

My life's fast merry-go-round
Was turning like a ceiling fan
As if the sky went underground,
As if our Almighty changed his plan
And angels realized they are hell-bound.

I am confused, I am in doubt,
I am forsaken by even a friendly crowd.
Even the most flattering self-portrait
Will not dismiss my premonition of the end;
Even the smartest critics won't interpret
My heartfelt verses sadly written in the sand.

My soul refused to shoulder
My nightmares through the years,
My daily burden is a heavy boulder
Of sleepless nights wrapped in sticky fears.

Today, my nightmares are behind,
We split. A well-foreseen divorce.
But she is always on my mind.
Remorse?

# Autumn Grieves

If I could be a god just for a day or two,
I would step down from the eternal blue.

I lived as if I was a savior of sinners
But realized it was in vain and risky;
I will be crucified by those who have been saved,
Even the road to the abyss is comfortably paved.

A glass of whiskey waits on the table,
My horse sneaked out of her stable
And grazes in the wilted grass
Under the gold and brass
Of the desolately falling leaves;
One life, two fates:
The early winter celebrates
When the late autumn grieves.

# Drumming Hooves

I play my weeping violin
As if I write my final verses,
But through the bitter tears
I push my happy laughter
And drumming hooves
Of four apocalyptic horses
Delaying our rest forever after.

I see the newer image of myself
Reflected in a crooked mirror:
Something between a devil and an elf,
Someone between a coward and a hero.

I cannot dance between the drops of rain,
I drag my feet like an exhausted tennis player,
I am a heavy truck that moved to a slow lane;
New life demands a fee; but I am not a payer.

# Hopes Fade

The sun has risen boldly faced,
The clouds gazed,
The horses grazed
The diamonds of morning dew,
I stirred my better hopes anew;
The clouds gazed,
Their shadows graced
Over the young green shoots
Under the shy emerging fruits.

The spring already sings and dances
I dared to take my half-baked chances
To prove that my best hopes will fade
If I will learn how sausages get made.

These days my interests are shifting,
I owe more, I own less,
I have to do a heavy lifting
Under the looming stress;
Life is a labyrinth, a maze,
I veer; I have no time to gaze.

I mow the grass and dig the trenches,
I never drink my Guinness in the pubs,
I sip from bottles thrown in the shrubs,
Then sleep and snore on dirty benches;
Quite often, cops lock me in a local jail
Where clocks move slower than a snail.

I am walking through a lifelong maze,
I blindly veer; I can no longer gaze...

# Secret Envelope

I reattached my wings,
I am not a fallen angel anymore.
My future sings:
"Unchain my heart
And set me free".
But no one hears my plea;
A lazy cupid aims his dart,
As if we are still in a state of war.

I sing the only song I know
Today, I want a better start:
"Unchain my heart
And let me go".

It is a final inning,
Life is exhausted and so am I,
No one is winning,
Our love ends in a dead hit.
My ego is well fostered, I am fit
To see my glowing future in the sky.

The wall between despair and hope
Cracked and collapsed;
I am calm, I am relaxed,
I know what's in the secret envelope.

I gazed into a jet-black night
Then closed my eyes to see the light.

# Trigger

Some ladies hate my caveman's manners,
Dislike my hairy chest with skull and bones;
The others like only the high-voiced tenors,
And yet majority desires much deeper baritones.

Four loudspeakers are reminding:
"When making love was just for fun,
Those days have gone..."
Only the classic songs forever binding
All those who are called "has-beens",
All those who still remember
The black-and-white and silent screens.

I am meticulously focused on everyday events,
And learn the worthy news from chitchat scholars:
Some people spitefully burn the dollars,
The others agonize and pinch the cents.

Our hatred grows big and bigger,
Nobody sees life eve to eye,
But keep their powder dry,
And often pull the trigger.

# Quagmires

For whom the willows wept
They wept for me.
I tried to reach my glee,
I drove along the time highways
Of smiles and pain,
In vain.
The globe turned like a ceiling fan,
Thrill never stopped, it simply left,
It passed me like a noisy train,
I plunged my toes in time, I ran.
I wanted to revive those days.

This planet is a merry-go-round,
My glee was never found:
I separated words from sentences,
And left no sounds in my music score,
I listened to a total silence,
Then morphed it to poetry galore.

The night throws its blinking stars
To drown in the whirlpools of the bars,
But like my old unsatisfied desires,
They are still sparkling in quagmires.

# Homage to Adolf Gottlieb

I had to miss the Sunday mass,
I sang the blues in my pajamas:
"Don't take me to your home,
I hardly am alive,
I am a useless old archive.
Don't run my heartbeat
With your metronome,
I am a sinking fleet."

My life is like a forgotten dream
That stubbornly evokes my run
From evil to a goodness' scream,
Under the lonesome frozen sun
Reflected in the mirror of your eyes,
Another willing hostage of despair,
Another victim of the eternity of ice.

Just like forgotten dream evokes
The Milky Way, our troubled world
Before the God's primordial word,
A spark of irresistible desire
Before the Big Bang and the fire.

# The Verdict

Hated by all and loved by none,
The death-judge spewed the verdict
The only one he learned by heart,
Which wasn't a surprise for anyone,
My friends and I already heard it
And tried to challenge it or outsmart.

I iron out wrinkles on my face
As if I pave the road to nowhere,
I am a blindfolded horse; I race
To make a circle from a square
And chase my luck on a merry-go-round.

As every old and dirty man
I think and talk only about death or sex;
I often get somebody spick-and-span
And in the morning sign the checks;
A centuries old comfy paradigm,
I have arrived into the pinnacle of time...

The fateful tree-tangled sky
Is hanging at my open window
Just like a quiet mourning widow
So gracefully stoic under stress
Wearing her modest lacy dress.

Fortieth day; my soul howls goodbye.

# Sacrifice

My eyes are not a source of solace,
Our unleashed days are virtually flawless,
Our cunning nights are habitually lawless,
Our emotions are constantly inept,
Because while devils worked
Our slothful wisdom slept,
Our ears were never perked.

We used to say,
Life is a sacrifice
And talk is cheap.
Some curse, some pray,
Life is a demon in disguise;
Time and again you sow,
The others reap.

# Proverbial Light

I have no buddies in my corner,
Sometimes an accidental mourner
May share a tear or heartfelt wishes.
After folks smoke cigars or sip cognac,
I wipe the floors and wash the dishes
Then feel like I am stretched on the rack.

Inside each strophe is a much better one,
It seems correct as long as I am writing,
I hope a cup of coffee brewed by dawn
Will let me scratch something exiting,
No morsel is too small
When poets are against the wall.

Another day arrives,
New happy and unhappy lives,
But I still write and write
In search of a proverbial light...

# Troubled Waters

My saint is good as he's always been,
I like this dedicated fella,
I keep his house clean,
For him I am a barefooted Cinderella.

Maybe I cast pearls before swine
Or give what's holy to the dogs,
Or kiss the sleeping frogs;
In any case, I sail the troubled waters
And teach some clumsy fathers
To make much better sons and daughters;
It is a noble, yet full of danger's task,
I have to wear a helmet and a mask.

I fail to tie the forms with connotations,
And dreadfully try in every speech
To introduce some sparkly alliterations
Like a new fur coat on to sunny beach...

To no avail, I drown in my desperations.

# Equilibriums Collapse

An alcoholic gulp, a barfly sips,
I am already loaded in my glee
And may escape the dire apocalypse
Or what the future has in store for me.
I never live a purpose-driven life
I never look beyond a daily strife.
I dive into the whirlpool of a change
Tomorrows look so harsh, so strange.

I squeezed some time
For my incurable obsession
With a few generous avengers.
They try to square the winners' circle,
But run from a remorseful confession
Into the nest of fallen, wingless angels.

The equilibriums collapse
My life is facing newest perils,
I am trying to avoid the traps,
But fall into the arms of devils.
Only the speed of my desire,
Only the pace of their decision
May set my measured life on fire
And leave me with a foggy vision.

My skepticism is growing far too fast,
The sun is hiding in the overcast;
I cherish my nocturnal world
Of painfully skinless sensibility,
Even a careless vulgar word
Highlights my birthright of nobility.

# Seven Paints

I play, no one keeps score,
The wisdom of the saints
Is not my shadow anymore;
My thoughts are darker than a crow,
My memory is muddy as a river flow
Which crawls under the bridge and faints,
Then resurrected as a rainbow's seven paints.

Life is a blindfolded drift,
A god-sent enigmatic gift
That kills and saves us all:
At times a minor lift,
At times, a major fall;
We take from Peter give to Paul,
We blow out the candles
To see the morning lights,
We start our daily scandals
Until a priest performs last rites,
Our final sacred apple-pie,
Before the hit of the abyss
Or sparkly orbits in the sky.

## Lead Me to Sunrise

Dawn is a burial of nights,
Dusk is a burial of lights.
Lead me to sunrise
That's ready to ascend
Or lead me to sunset
That's waiting to descend.
Lead me to the exit from a lifelong maze
Then walk me to the end of days...

# Life Cries

I didn't reach the Promised Land,
I am still living in its foyer;
My life is passing by like a marching band
Playing the ancient country tunes
Known to Becky Thatcher and Tom Sawyer
And echoed in the bullet-riddled saloons.

Even my love asks to be born,
My heart is destined to be torn.

Life cries: "If you don't like adventures,
Get out of my way,
I have no time to waste,
I am a waterfall of ventures
With the most intriguing taste.
I am like an art museum
Of high-brow masterpieces
And low-brow modern morsels;
I am the gladiators' colosseum
Filled with the human faces
And the most popular immortals.
Just walk through me; I have it all
But walk, don't ever crawl."

# Crispy Leaves

I waited for the swirling leaves
To touch the wilted grass;
I wept, I closed my eyes,
I couldn't handle the demise
Of the late autumn's melted brass.

I heard the tarnished sun:
Another winter has begun.

I walked over still crispy leaves
Between the lonely naked trees;
They stood like sleepless guards
Protecting Mother-nature's
Seldom-visited graveyards.

# Backbiting Dragnet

I am not bloodthirsty, I was drafted,
I simply went into the grinder
Which the warmongers crafted...
Allow me a minuscule reminder:
Only the fallen saw the end of war;
I luckily escaped the final score.

So many moons have passed,
I am back in Vietnam at last:
As in the tortured past,
I walk along the fields of rice and grain,
As in the bloody past,
I am pierced by the darts of endless rain;
The sun surrounded to overcast;
I walk and whisper: I miss my brothers,
I don't miss the pain.
Vietnam is not a magnet,
It is a backbiting dragnet
That rakes the ugly, bad and good,
And lets us pick under our own hood.

# Futile Strive

The delicately colored autumn sky
Looks artfully handcrafted
Or lustrously painted by the angels...
Only the color blinded strangers
Who are abruptly passing by
Without being lured or even drafted
Into the constant futile strive
Between the beautiful and vile,
At least from eight to five,
Just for a while.

# A Showboat

It as a devastating treason,
Reality betrayed my trust
In history's axiomatic truth-
Not every boat was lifted by a tide;
There is no scientific reason,
I easily can prove it if I must.

I threw away illusions of my youth,
My fragile innocence forever died.

Those who were born to crawl
Will never learn to fly,
They see a wall, give up and cry.
Some boats can't float and sink,
I am a showboat: I travel, eat and drink.

# Saint Paul

Paul is a saint
I am named after,
My Mom deserves the blame;
Paul was concerned
And chose to faint
When learned
That I don't like my name,
De facto.

He claimed he heard the Lord
In his nightmare
Taking nap close to Damascus;
He was not one of those eleven
Who followed Jesus Christ;
He never asked us,
But prearranged himself to heaven
Near those so cruelly sacrificed.

Besides, his venomously angry letters
Divided Christians and Jews,
Agnostic sceptics and trendsetters,
And others with their unfamiliar views.

Paul's deeds initiated our never-ending,
Devouring and fruitless bloody strife,
Therefore, each one of us forever after
Became a tragic fighter or a crafty actor
On the stage of life.

## Intellectual Hierarchy

It's hard to be the best in class,
My buddies constantly demanded
What is this? Vas ist das?
I had to know yesterday,
I had to foresee tomorrows,
And all between the Milky Way
And Andromeda's swirly flows.

My Porsche runs on wine and cheese,
The future has already happened.
After my eggs-and-bacon breakfast
I ran against a morning chilly breeze.
Meanwhile the heavy clouds blackened
And raindrops justified and proved
The newest theory of strings;
A minute later vivid lightning rods
Embraced existence of the gods,
And the resounding arrival of Big bang
Brought by the vibrating animated rings.

I used to be the best in class,
I still hear echoed vas ist das.

The hierarchy among the major intellects
Doesn't require the creepy side effects;
One easily climbs higher on that ladder
After succeeds in emptying his bladder.

# My Four Leaf Clover

My boson friend seems to presage
The imminence of his own death in war.
I didn't write the final page,
I still cast a long shadow on the floor.

Our days swirl like an ancient carousel,
Meanwhile we ride the wooden horses,
And make these aimless rounds.
Life is an unfinished symphony,
A boundless collection of the sounds
Predestined disappear in infamy,
But we will hear the warning bells…
For whom they toll?
This time they toll for someone else.

I picked my four leaf lucky clover,
I am still alive; another war is over.
Cacophony and dissonance ascend
And morph into a pleasing harmony
Even for the best of us,
Who live with premonition of a bitter end.

# Sea Change

My angel-savior is just a cunning ghost,
Even today he is off somewhere,
Although, today I need him most,
But once again, he didn't hear my prayer.

A glass of vodka on the table,
The moon is hanging near my gable;
Only the crooked mirrors
Knew the secrets of my troubled youth,
Only our fallen heroes knew,
But took with them the truth.

Don't ever try to read my mind,
There is nothing left for you.
My death sentence is already signed,
I am just waiting in a lifelong queue.

I was politely "Krogered"
And put my trophies on the seat:
A bottle of Italian red
And a nicely marbled cut of meat,
Then started my capricious car,
I live not very far.

Suddenly someone turned the switch
And started the incredible sea change:
The parking lot became a firing range
And I was rescued by a flying witch...
The outcome no one could prearrange;
The art of living morphed into a kitsch.

A silent pause hangs in the room,
I wouldn't dare to say a word,
A wicked witch is flying on her broom,
I am entirely hypnotized by this absurd;
Even after she flew away bliss-bound,
I couldn't make single sound.

The end of times?
Not if you read my rhymes.

# Custodian

Despite the plentitude of proof,
I bail my young and impish relatives
Who are not too friendly with the law;
It is my personal imperative
To keep alive the status quo
And let them stay away from prisons...
I am like a rain that knocks on every roof
Just as a habit with some foggy reasons;
I am a custodian of my family affairs
I try to get the musical three-legged chairs
For my unleashed and undeserving heirs.

# Laissez-faire

The end of a weary night,
The start of a new dawn,
I missed that pretty sight,
The draperies were drawn.

We actually were born
In our feisty childhoods:
We were cut out, chiseled,
Shaped and taught to fight;
Our naiveté was torn,
Then left behind forlorn
Somewhere in the woods.

I guess, it was injected in my veins:
My live-and-let-live attitude
Keeps me above the daily feud,
And safe from being screwed
By those who occupy a higher chair,
And yet, my motto still remains
The ancient "Laissez-faire!"

# Enigmatic Painting

Life is an enigmatic painting,
Starkly photorealistic,
Consuming but frustrating
And yet, impeccably holistic.

Life is a bomb of yesterday,
A pacifier for today,
A yardstick for tomorrows,
The arrows flying from the bows
Into the trust that didn't last,
A reassurance that quickly passed.

A naughty morning breeze
Tries to resolve our problems
Under the golden candelabrums
Of color changing autumn trees,
Under the heavy leafy branches,
Under the brassy patches
Of lightly trembling leaves
Like red-faced yellow-bellied thieves
Fretfully waiting on the justice benches.

Is it a time to live,
A time to kill,
A time to give,
A time to take,
A time to wake
And ask for a refill?

## Passion

I trust the rumors,
I thrash the news,
I quash the baby boomers,
The cobblers never have good shoes.

I wouldn't kill a fiery passion in my heart
From water-hoses filled with prayers,
I want to resurrect a well-forgotten art
Of fighting with the militant naysayers.

I entered life too late,
I never had much time,
I rushed, I didn't wait;
I didn't play it safe,
I looked for cracks
In every paradigm.

The wingless angels worked on me,
Nose-dived and failed to save.
I knew my soul will live in glee,
I knew that history prefers the brave

# Underdog

It is a golden autumn evening,
The tired sun drops from the sky,
My court is full, no one is leaving,
Nobody says goodbye.

My lawyer tries to win acquittal,
And shows off my pedigree:
My predecessors' stones and crosses.
The jury seems completely noncommittal,
But curious enough to learn a recipe
For centuries of our victories and losses.

And then their envy dumped on me
The fastest guilty verdict in the world;
My dream about days of glee
Fell on its own sword.
I felt like an ill-fated underdog,
I stood entirely broken-hearted;
My lawyer tried to dump a log
But only farted.

My more expensive lawyer
Calmly said, she will appeal;
Of course, I couldn't disagree;
The bail money set me free
And I awaited a much better deal.

I'll make the longest poem short:
She won, we beat the goddamn court.

# Blue and Red

No one will carry you
From one life to another;
No one will ever force you
To fly into the eternity of blue;
If you don't want, don't bother.

No one will ever push you
Into the fiery no-way-out red;
Don't ever cry: "I was misled."

You prayed for twelve and cast the dice,
Life knew the value. You knew the price.

We all will die and never see the sun,
Let all the others cry after we are gone.

# Sediment

The end was evident,
There was no wine,
Just muddy sediment
Dwelled in the bottle of my life,
Like a forgotten wartime mine
Or a postcard from my ex-wife.

At night, all cats seem black:
Whether I am lying flat
Or flying like a vampire bat.
Even if I never meow
But learned to quack,
Even if I never moo
Like an abandoned cow
But like a dog begin to bark.
The sun will always rise
Even above my trailer park
To flaunt the diamonds of morning dew
Even the timid end of life restarts anew.

Only at night all cats seem black…

# Evolution

Time won: my views ceased to exist:
For me it was the deadliest mass murder,
For time in was just a victorious debate,
I grouped my intellectual debris,
And said, revenge can wait
Then ordered a gigantic triple burger.

Am I cocooned or tightly wrapped?
Did I outlive my humble mind?
Am I self-righteous or inept
And left my curiosity behind?
Did I calm down just enough
To fall into a long-range love?

There is no cure for existential dread,
I wonder if I'll ever get my daily bread.

I never was too small, never too mighty,
I never felt is if I was an underdog,
I longed for the most gorgeous goddess Aphrodite,
And even that prince was just a once-kissed frog.

I am a freelance dreamer,
I dared to ask our Redeemer:
"Do you believe in evolution?"
He said: "For all your mortal sins
It is the only highly valuable solution.
But even I on one occasion failed:
I couldn't walk the Sea of Galilee,
I sailed."

# Refugee

The colorful fluorescent tubes
Create strobe-lighted optical illusions
Of the New-York dazzling sense of thrill
Under the shower of spheres and cubes,
Along the most incredible confusions
Between our resentment and goodwill.

I am a Broadway diver,
I am a refugee; I am a taxi driver;
I leave my youth in the rearview mirrors
I leave my life's past tenses in the dust,
I leave deserters and the fallen heroes
To dwell on my acceptance and mistrust;
But those who occupy my cab's back seat,
Will march with me to the Big Apple beat...

## Confession

I painted bubbly urban women,
I painted elegantly cubbish men,
I was a cupid-hooker of the arts:
You paid; I gladly aimed my darts.

# Wake Up Your Master

We hide from a singing swan,
Most likely clumsy or fictitious;
The same goes on
With our ambitions:
We like only the summits
We cannot reach,
We like the laws that we can breach.

Hey, angels, wake up your master
Then He may talk to us more often
And admit that he created a disaster.
Even the Commandments didn't help,
In vain, we roll our eyes and yelp,
But neither He nor his muffled saints
Acknowledge our complaints,
Therefore, we'll follow our own beat
And try to dump our religious chains.

Whether we invented a role model
Or were created by His word,
I will uncork my Irish Whisky bottle
And cut the never needed cord.

# A Guiltless Breath

I turn the key
And start a car
Or open a tight door
To hear somebody from afar
Who says "Make love, not war!"

Only the limits of imagination
And fears of downstairs cremation
Don't let me see the light upstairs;
I can't defeat a fire in my soul
Unless I use a water hose
That pours my hopes and prayers.

I have no chronic dread of death,
She has no key into my universe;
I want the fragile value of my verse
To match a baby's guiltless breath.

I can't get out
From where I haven't been.
There is no certainty I wouldn't doubt,
There is no nightmare I haven't seen.

I reached my glowing independence

# A Little Fish

Aquarius the famous water-bearer
Was young and not too clever,
The boy carried his water in a cup
Enough to drink but not to grow up.

I've read the fables that were canonized,
Sometimes, I've read between the lines
And noticed all those sugar-coated lies.
The ages passed, no one apologized;
At times, there were some scientific finds,
But we believe traditions, not our minds;
We rarely trust our own ears and eyes,
And never pay attention to the warning signs.

When I was poor I tried to hide from creditors...
My small aquarium was rented by a cute goldfish,
She didn't have a pied a terre to run from predators.
My little fish was swimming a few days tongue-tied,
She didn't breathe; she turned her belly up and died...

My squeamish cat is staring at the empty dish.

# Petals Falling

I didn't bring from wars my spoils,
I didn't bring from wars my trophies,
My only worthy valuables
Were nuggets of my strophes.

It is much more than meets the eye:
The body piercing rains are pouring,
The earsplitting thunders also roaring,
The weary sun falls from the sky,
Even the leaves and petals falling,
But we are still together: you and I.

I play my tunes on the strings of rain
The broken mirrors of my soul
Don't show faces of my fallen heroes,
They rest in peace and feel no pain,
They aimed but didn't reach the goal.

My heartbeat trudges through my veins,
My life is bravely galloping
Under the heaven's canopy,
And I am the one who holds the reigns.

## Piercing Hearts

I used to be a flying cupid
And even wrote a lovely book
"The art of piercing hearts";
I knew how to aim my darts.

I wasn't gullible and stupid,
I didn't preach the Holy Bible
To the corrupted prison guards.
I whistled past their lousy boneyards.

The lawyers won't justify their crimes
With why-they-have-done-it reasons;
They weepily count months and seasons
While I am writing these heartfelt rhymes.

I hate the wardens and the prison guards,
I am one of those feel-pain angered bards
Who never glorify those adolescent strifes
That try to save the death row killers' lives.

## Diamonds of Dew

I still remember, her eyes were clear
Like sparkling diamonds of morning dew,
Green like malachite of springtime grass.
Her gentle voice was like a quiet whisper
Of the leaves awakened by a breeze.

I still remember the most vibrant symphony
Piercing the church's stained glass,
And the amazing opulence
Of a wedding service wrapped around us.

I still remember the red-hot promises
And wishes that slid into eternal freeze.
I seldom travel through the provinces
And asked to say the famous "cheese".

Forgiveness is a long-forgotten art,
Our so-called happy marriage fell apart.

# Forever Drunk

A shorter second hand jumps nervously
On a dial of my old-fashioned watch
Like a barefoot walker on the sunlit beach
Instead of drinking a smooth Irish scotch.

We are forever drunk
But our conscience smiles
As a great symbol of approval;
And if you dare to look in our eyes
You will see the disapproving ice,
Totally pitiless and awfully cruel.

When my old-fashioned watch stops ticking,
The sun still rises and the rays are pricking;
The nights keep falling on the ground,
The darker forces dance around.

My blue-eyed innocence
Arrived too late to my uneasy life,
And brings on yet another vicious strife,
And once again I have to grab the falling knife.

## Above the Clouds

Above the clouds,
There are no loud crowds,
And no dilapidated city flats,
No coffins and no shrouds,
No hockey sticks, no baseball bats;

Above the clouds
I met only the wingless angels,
I met only the foes and strangers.

Above the clouds,
I met infinity of seven mortal sins,
No David's stars, no crosses;
It was a melting pot of hollow wins
And massive losses.

I want to be exactly six feet under,
No lightning rods, no thunder.
I want to be a centerpiece,
I want to rest in peace
Below the clouds…

# She

She unexpectedly appeared
Just like a ray of early dawn;
It seemed as if a path was cleared
And all of us were gone.

She flirted briefly with the press
Exporting a firmly frozen smile;
She picked the apple of success
And chewed it for a while.

A star will never spark
Unless the sky is dark.

# Bourgeoisie

My morbid loneliness
Pulls off my safety blanket and bedsheets,
And takes me to the streets,
I melt into the crowds,
I lose my confidence but keep the doubts.

All of a sudden, we are one and faceless,
We are so-called bourgeoisie,
Something between despair and glee,
Between a cup of coffee and a banquette.

## Ascension

When life is paused
And doors are locked,
The future quietly but timely knocks;
Meanwhile each ad in my mailbox
Assaults me unopposed
Although my gun is always cocked.

My guiding angel walks across the sky,
I scream and wave my coat,
He doesn't pay attention;
He whistles requiem
And doesn't miss a single note...

I am losing interest in my ascension.

# The Four

We hide from the Apocalyptic Four,
The red, the black, the pale, the white;
But we are searching for the other four,
For each unamiable right:
Life, liberty, equality and happiness
And often wind up in a silent emptiness.

From dusk to down
There are no dramas and no thrills,
We are frustrated, bored and yawn,
We merely pay our daily bills.

The wingless angels
Don't descend, they simply fall;
They are just futile strangers
In my grief-stricken soul.

Our ancient saints were worshiped
From dawn to dusk,
Today, their wings were clipped
Their glory dwindled in the husk;
We can no longer trust in you,
Our almighty man-created Lord,
We are not standing in a queue
To hear your word.

We'd rather hear the deafening Big Bang,
We'd rather hear the bells that rang;
They rang for you and me,
For those who are set forever free.

# Withered petals

We are the ruined and abandoned dams
We are naïve and unsuspecting lambs
Led heartlessly to a bloody slaughter,
We are the babies tossed with the water.

The generals were loaded with the medals
While we were serving as a cannon fodder.
Today, we are the fallen withered petals,
A comfy path to bliss for a willing plodder.

# I wrote that book

Don't fall from riches to the world of rags,
Don't fight the powerful and moneybags;
Just judge your cheeses by the rinds,
They are not devils in disguise.
I won my bid to write a tell-all book
About a steely-eyed owner of the winds,
A shameless and untrustworthy crook,
A waterfall of malicious and longwinded lies.

I wrote that book,
I didn't let him off the hook,
He smirked and promised to respond:
He is in jail, but winds don't blow anymore
Across my Granny's pond,
I won a battle, lost the war,
I had to dock my sailboat,
Nobody buys the book I wrote.

It is a story of my troubled life,
I grabbed another falling knife.

# The Rider of a Unicorn

I am on the path of least resistance,
I am the troubled rider of a unicorn,
I am concerned about my existence,
After the red sunsets, I am forlorn.

I am at peace in the world of terrors,
I am like a flowerbed of daisies
Surrounded by poison ivy
Of seldom unintended errors,
By the shaky equilibrium of crazies
Sometimes distasteful but lively.

War only killed my sins and virtues,
The tooting bullets pierced my body,
A nurse could see the light of day;
For us the wars are damned and bloody,
Only for generals it may be glamorous.
I am alive; I am a resurrected Lazarus,
I am not John the Baptist,
My head is not forgotten on a silver tray.
Today, I am a sinless life-imitating artist.

I see no glory in being covered
With stars and stripes,
In being timely rediscovered
By the uncaring undertaker types,
Or by the cowardly jingoistic hawks
In their self-serving xenophobic talks.

# Pine Top Casket

My head began to sound like a choir
That needs a skilled conductor
I bet, my morbid brains conspire
To make out of me a patient or a doctor.

I know how sausages are made,
I even know how kids are born;
My future hopelessly decayed
Before my soul gets airborne.

My mind wants me to take some pills
To cure my allergies and other ills,
Or find a good job and make more dough;
But I am not lazy, I hardly ever sleep
And make enough to pay my bills.
I was not born to reap,
I only like to sow.

My soul's half-empty basket,
My body's pine-top casket
Will find stairway to bliss,
Some others hit-and-miss.

## Our Fates

Life doesn't require imagination of a mind,
I can foresee a boring cookie cutter ripple,
Each clones each other and expends in kind
The mirror images of valleys, hills and peoples.
I live within this tiresome exhibition
Of my creator's unjustified ambition.

My confidence completely disappears:
I measure time by days and weeks,
I measure life by months and years,
At nights I count hours and minutes,
But can't achieve what my imagination seeks,
I am terrified, I reached my limits.

And yet, the sun will also rise
And I may outlast my own demise.

At least, I outlived the fallen heroes,
I cannot see their faces in the mirrors,
They can no longer share their stories,
Their pompous joys and timid worries...
The heroes vanished past the gates,
Even the gods can't change our fates.

## Picasso

Most artists see the sun
But paint a yellow yolk,
The gifted paint the sun
Even when they see the yolk.

I need someone to follow
I have no innovative visions,
The fruits of wisdom hang quite low,
And make for me my own decisions.

Pablo Picasso cynically announced:
"A mediocre artist always imitates,
A giant arrogantly steals"
His wisdom was denounce
By the half-baked beginners,
Right from the boat or out of the gates.
And by the pompous talking heads,
Riding their cars much bigger wheels.

We used to say, heads over heels

# The Rest Is Silence

It is not a sought after end.
I acted like a Greek immortal
With acumen and prudence
No one could understand.
I only saw red, blue and purple
And taught my trusting students
To drink a lot and never pray.

Gods will refill our empty glasses,
They always brush aside our sins
Then gift us an undeserved forgiveness,
The demagoguery of organized religions,
The real opium for the devoured masses
Injected into the minds of human pigeons.
Instead of healing our chronic moral illness,
They flaunt our sporadic futile wins.

I am sick; I drag my feet like a tired dancer,
Who asked the ill-famed Hamlet's question,
But doesn't expect a comprehensive answer,
Explaining the tragic legacy of my depression.

Something is rotten in the state of Denmark,
The rest is silence under a rainbow arc.

# Touch His Face

Even in a total brightness
Of a front-row seat,
I doubt my saints' rightness,
And beg for trick or treat.

The freezing rain
Whispers to my ears:
"Forget your pain,
Forget your fears,
No one believes,
Pull out aces from your sleeves
And play the honest game,
Whether you lose or win
The world will stay the same,
Committing every known sin
In the pursuit of wealth or fame.

Don't trust the crooked mirrors,
There are no birthright heroes.
Don't lose your grace
Under the daily stress.
God knows your address,
He'll allow you to touch His face."

## Weaker Link

I even tasted courage in a brutal war,
But wisdom locked from me its door:
Erratically, I am sober or use a shrink,
But then I gratefully sink into my drink.

I used a straw to sip my mother's milk,
I tried to rearrange my drinking habits,
My DNA refused to fix its weaker link,
My hat is empty; no more rabbits.

# Tumbledown Shrouds

I tried but couldn't forgive and pray,
I shelved my answers till a better day.
Quite often faith, hope and even love
Are stunned by our never-ending bluff.

The moons crawled through the skies,
The clouds bumped into each other,
The angels couldn't stop our sins and lies
After a forsaken son has risen to his father.

The modern kings don't serve their gods,
They never abdicate their golden thrones,
They use the cannon fodder and the drones,
We fight against the overwhelming odds.

I wrote this epigram
Before the crowd killed another lamb.
Ever so often,
I can forestall without any doubts
They'll bury me not in a coffin,
But wrapped in tumbledown shrouds.

# Wrong Side Up

My life begins to crater
And as a historian would say:
"He owned a restaurant;
Today, he is a waiter,
But has more time to flaunt
And much more time to pray."

A coexistence with my conscience
Has a huge pile of clever rules
Which I amend but not ignore;
It is a convoluted game of chess
Played my a pair of stubborn mules
Both try at once to get into a narrow door.

I spent a few amusing days and nights
In a picturesque deserted seaside town,
A visual insanity of my came true dreams;
Even my boring life turned upside-down:
The real world is not exactly as it seems,
The moon creates the lights,
The sun reflects the beams.

The roots of the inverted trees
Scratch a soft belly of the sky,
As if I rest, wrong side up, in peace,
But even the gods don't know why.

# Choppy Past

I wrote a page of prayers,
The last one in my lifelong book,
And saw my soul in God's crosshairs,
I can no longer linger in my modest nook.

My thoughts predict tomorrows,
My poems justify the choppy past,
I veer between my joys and sorrows,
Surrounded with doubts that forever last.

I locked my pretty castle in the sky,
There are too many human dinosaurs,
I didn't want to share my apple pie
With those who're walking on all fours.

I wrote the final page,
The page of rage,
The page of doom,
But under a nom de plume.

# Adventures Ended

A messenger of death,
An old proverbial canary...
She's read my shy obituary,
I gave away my final breath.

My life's adventures ended.
I asked the faultless Lord,
My genuinely trusted friend:
Why after your son ascended
To the infinity of bliss,
The rest of us only descend
Into the fiery abyss?

## Iron Bars

I wonder who is jailed
The mighty Lord or I.
I look at the ceaseless sky
Dissected by the iron bars
And see a dreamy ocean
I never sailed.
The Lord looks back at me
Across the same old bars
And thinking in reverse:
That I am absolutely free
To heal my wartime scars
And to reshape this verse.

# Primavera

Am I still fighting windmills
That loom above my universe?
Do I still try to cure our ills
With clout of my wicked verse?

I am in Florence rejoicing Primavera,
Another indecisive spring.
The Dome still towering
Above the multilingual crowds,
Above the masterpieces
Of Brunelleschi, Donatello and Masaccio
Wrapped in my poetic shrouds
And thoughts of Dante and Boccaccio.

It is not a big surprise,
It is a forever open door,
I've seen it many times before;
It doesn't blow up my skirt
As my ex-wife would say.
It is a sweet dessert,
It is a sunny gorgeous day
Reflected in the Arno River,
Slicing the town like a cleaver

I have a cozy feeling of déjà vu
The gods already pedaled my canoe.

## Dulcet Voices

I froze; I didn't have a clue,
Life dared to cast the dice;
She knew the value,
I hardly guessed the price.

Dreaded by all but loved by none,
Fate climbed the tower of aggressions,
Our obsessions with The Son
And other tendencies are gone;
There is no born-again and no rerun:
I feel the sad futility of my remorse
And gloom of my deceitful confessions.

I hear the irritating urban noises
Of downtown's busy afternoons,
And yet, I hear the dulcet voices
And the most easy-going tunes.

# Blindfolded

I've read the ancient tea leaves,
But disagreed with their predictions;
Too many tragedies and griefs,
Too many feisty contradictions.

The sky is crying,
As in the film, I am dancing in the rain;
Meanwhile, the fallen angel flies again
And guides my daily needs,
Thus I am blindfolded in the weeds.

Where is the Promised Land?
Where is the happy end?
Only the sacrificial lamb has risen,
My soul and flesh are still in prison.

The piercing winds already blow,
I wonder if the gentle virgin snow
Will dance above the wicked streams
And freeze the innocence of dreams.

## Insane

I have my New Year wishes
If I decide to change my life,
Meanwhile, I wash the dirty dishes
In smoky joints of my unending strife.

Reality doesn't resonate in me,
It is just written in my fate,
It is a leafless, useless tree,
It is a breakfast served too late.

A guiding angel is my soul's copilot,
He tries to lead me through the world,
I cannot comprehend his every word,
Nor have I skills to download or file it.

This world is too arcane,
Just like the modern art,
And yet I am the true insane
Among the insanely smart.

Some wingless angels drown in a lake,
Just like the ordinary people,
I hopelessly search for a lucky break,
I try to get a little bit of glee in every ripple.

Carved on my heart, scarred on my skin,
Locked in my soul, devoured by my brain...
Perhaps I am insane, perhaps I am wrong,
But I still write and sing my own song.

# Breaking News

I left my birthplace town just to be there,
I gave away my crown just to be fair,
I found love just to forget,
I clowned all my live just to regret.

What's easier, to live or to be dead?
The living work to get their daily bread,
The fallen rest in peace, instead.

It's easier to teach a horse to sing,
Than to undress a naked king,
It's easier to ask a bull to dance on ice,
Than for a snake to close its eyes
Or for a poet to enter paradise.

I ran from the guidelines' cleaver
Into the critics' merciless jaws,
Only inseparable good and evil
Suspected who I was.

The heavens got the blues:
You sold a single book, my agent sad,
A local TV put it in the breaking news,
I didn't care, I went to bed.

# Frailty

I guess, it was a frailty of age,
I left my comfortable golden cage
At a rather reasonable time,
And jumped into obscurity of the unknown,
My eager curiosity was thrown
On altars of the established paradigms.

I piled my sins, my failures and defeats
Then climbed this trembling obelisk
To see the garden of a much better life
Without risking glory of my daily strife.

I saw the Holy Gate,
I saw my namesake waits
For his pal Peter to turn the key
And let me enter the eternal glee
Before I changed my guarded mind.

I am still hovering above humankind.

# Hot and Red

My life is like a film with a well-known ending,
My premonition is contrary to common sense,
As if I am on the hopeless mission
To catch a real truth beyond the fence;
My searches failed to lay an egg...
Some have a life, I simply hold a bag.

I tamed my wild desire,
Today, I am conformist,
I drown in my middleclass quagmire,
I drown in the human fruitless mist.

A life will disappear tonight
After I fall asleep,
Wrapped in the blinding light;
The gods will take my parting breath,
Even my guiding angels will not weep,
When I embrace my charming death.

My life was climbing by a cheery slope,
But I could see that light is hot and red.
The gods will wish, the saints will hope,
While I will be in hell and infinitely dead.

# Horse Trading

When a blind leads a blind,
Both fall into a nasty pit...
A leader could be jailed,
The other could be only fined,
The juries pick whom to acquit,
And whom to leave behind.

The globe is still revolving,
The humans are evolving
Into the species yet unknown;
I trust, they will accept the Bang
As our cornerstone.

Why does the blinding sun
Descends and lets the joyless moon
Remind that some of us are gone
Into a better life,
Where no one needs a silver spoon.

Long shadows clothed the skies,
The stubborn moon refused to glow
And bargained with sunrise,
Both flourished in horse trading...
Meanwhile the lights are fading,
I must go.

# Undying Sun

It is too early for a rainbow,
The hurricane is still alive
And only my angels know
That like a bee I lost my hive.

Confused religious aspirations
Kept me away from realizing
That I desolately failed,
I lived, but the will to live has died.
I veered along the shaky foundations,
While the undying sun was rising
And my tomorrow was unveiled:
No fear, no greed, no vanity, no pride.

I drank, I ate, I paid,
I loved, I hated and I played
I went through opened and closed doors,
I went through miserable wars,
I slayed, I didn't aim to please.
Do I deserve to rest in peace?

A broken chair
On a dirty floor
Unknown to a broom,
A dense and stinky air
Of a dusty room;
That's what I left behind,
Besides a peace of mind
And a self-effacing tomb.

## Absurd Decision

Love at the first sight,
Immediate intense attraction,
A blinding light, immense delight,
A great reality against abstraction.

I carefully watched everything
With my twenty-twenty vision,
I saw on her my wedding ring,
A termination of my absurd decision.

I saw my foes, I saw my friends,
I saw the happy and the tragic ends.

I separated words from sentences,
I threw the notes from music score,
And listened to the vacuum of senses,
But heard my songs and poetry galore.

I reached my greatest masterpiece,
I can no longer write; I rest in peace.

# Merciless Jaws

I am awfully bored and lonely,
Just like a bedbug in an empty bed,
Completely bleak and homely
Just like an unwanted wilted bread.

I tried my utmost best:
I wrote about women I caressed,
About virtues in my mortal sins,
About losses in my frequent wins,
About crimes I jokingly confessed,
About broken hearts in my affairs,
About pleasures and despairs,
And all the rest...

I didn't hide under a nom de plume,
I smashed the mirrors in my room.

Only inseparable good and evil
Suspected who I truly was,
I ran from the bystanders' cleaver
Into the critics' merciless jaws.

# Afterglow

It is my inborn urge to learn and know,
It is my search of the evasive afterglow,
It is not a foggy drift,
It is a pain of disillusions,
It is a lullaby for my confusions,
It is a god sent unexpected gift.

My eager and relentless curiosity
Led me to each obvious monstrosity,
I tried to calm or iron certain quarrels,
I mostly used my mind; at times, a gun,
Unfortunately, those days have gone,
Today, I am just resting on my laurels.

My efforts seem attractive in retrospect,
The ancient habits were preserved,
The modern matters weren't wrecked,
The reasons saved and wisdom served.

# Final Nail

My coffin threw away its final nail,
And like a boat unfurled its sail,
I am blinded by the rising sun,
The final journey has begun.

Time has conceded its defeat,
My mind gets younger every day,
The church's bells don't ring;
My tires and highways meet
And joyfully sing:
If there is a will, there is a way.

My conscience whispers to my ear:
"You had a stunning life well spent;
I wonder if somebody drops a tear,
When noticing that you went."

# The Human Pile

The physical reality of death
Is a chilling image of a parting breath
Reflected in the minds of living;
It is a lifetime game
Lost long before the final inning,
And nobody is here to blame.

No one will wear my shoes
And walk my so-called extra mile,
I met nobody who may choose
To float as an abandoned lonely isle.

Even the perverted priests teach us
That we must never stand alone,
And coexist with others in the human pile;
Even the one who's dumped under the bus
Before his name is chiseled in the stone
Which marks his soul's confinement and exile
Surrounded with the belligerence of strangers
Veiled as the diligence of gentle fallen angels.

## Two Apples

There were two apples
On the Wisdom tree;
We are familiar with the first,
The tasty apple of our carnal knowledge.
The second was the apple of contention,
The apple which created bloody wars
And a fragile, never lasting peace.

Those apples were two unknown chapels
They were forever cursed
As opioids for the masses
And keep our guiltless souls
From the ascension
Into the open golden doors,
Into infinity of the promised bliss.

## Forever Stoned

I learned to drink and sleep alone,
Without peers, without neighbors;
These lonely nights and days
As if it is my blanket, my comfort zone;
It is that cherished time
When I can rest in peace
And get awakened by the rattling sabers.

I stand alone just like a king dethroned,
I am a proud cornerstone forever stoned.

# Trinity

Who is that expert sailor
Who will navigate our ship
Over eternity of dire weather?
Who is that perfect tailor
Who may stitch us all together?

Please, ring the bells,
They will be heard
Across meridians and parallels;
Not only by the Third
But by the Second
And the First.

I trust, the Holy Trinity
Will satisfy our thirst
For paradise,
For its infinity
If we will ever rise.

# A Roman Goddess

LA; I stood among the curious bystanders,
A loud bunch of oily packed sardines
Or rather tightly parked old cars
With the scratched, bent and rusty fenders.

She was a famous actress,
Tall, gorgeous and well-dressed;
She moved like a majestic swan
Caressed by the early loving dawn.

She had a figure of a Roman goddess,
Full, slightly twisted and coldblooded.
She noted, I undressed her with my eyes;
She was young and willing, I was immodest,
And our vast imagination flooded
With love desires and devils in disguise.

A constant story of my life,
I was afraid to catch a falling knife

# Drawbridge

I used to be a stranger in the labyrinths of love,
I hovered as a hawk, not as a frightened dove,
And when I couldn't see my prey,
I would just make a circle and fly away.

All of a sudden, I truly fell in love,
And realized, my heart and flesh is not enough.
I had a plane, a yacht and a good-looking house;
She planned to capture all of the above
And leave me poor as the church's mouse.

I found a quick exit from the labyrinths of love,
I am not a stranger in love ventures anymore,
I am still slowly sliding from the ridge
But I am neither hawk nor dove...
I sadly lost the most important war:
I failed to close the carnal-minded drawbridge.

# Wish

The darkest night
Arrives before a dawn,
The brightest day
Enjoys its afternoon.
There is no end in sight,
It is about four or five,
The fight is dragging on,
Only a few are still alive
In my platoon.

The shadows of the dead
Cross the Elysian Fields,
The resting place of our souls
According to the Dead Sea scrolls:
Where our lies remain unsaid,
Where no one uses swords or shields,
Where no one ever knelt or bowed,
Where sorrows never ebbed or flowed.

Life is a battlefield
Where every one of us
Is either a predator or prey;
Time runs and wouldn't yield,
We choke under the coexistence' bus,
Nobody bought a seat above the fray.

My savior is busy,
He walks on water,
And feeds us with the fish.

We take it easy:
He died and was resurrected...
That what is after our slaughter
We may only humbly wish.

## No Clues

Some reach their goals
Of being rich without college,
The others saved their souls
And gained true knowledge.

The sirens go off
And warn our minds:
"Pull your tomorrow
From the trough,
Connect the dots,
And hone your finds".

We wonder if we see our hearts
Reflected in the broken mirrors,
Or there are our broken hearts
Crushed by the careless heroes.

Even the nosy have no clues,
No recognizable footprints,
No witnesses, no hints.
Only the futile local news.

# Looming Storm

I fell from the cast-iron pan
Into the merciless, hungry fire,
I fell from the high tightrope
Into a bottomless quagmire,
I fell from glory of a happy man
Into a dire despair without hope.

I spent some time with the devil in the slums,
We shared some stories, drinks and eats,
We liked to hear each other's drums,
But always marched to our own beats.

I won't confess my sins in later memoirs,
They were acknowledged and forgiven,
Or drowned in my drinks across the bars;
In any case, the devil and I are squarely even.

I watched the looming storm,
The winds were heavy but lukewarm,
The thick gray clouds blocked the sun,
The chirping birds have gone,
My dog is scared but barks,
The lightning briskly sparks,
The thunder wildly roars,
I went inside and shut the doors.

My devil marched into the storm,
No one has seen him anymore.

# Fated Time

I like to taste my fated time,
I chew the hours and days,
I live to eat, to drink, and rhyme
My thoughts in every written phrase.

I am a captive of this old routine,
I am a hostage of these treasures;
I am a rusty but often used machine
For my devout readers' pleasures.

My verse is a painting with a rough surface,
A symphony with flashes of a vivid color;
My verse is rambling in the unknown places
Like hounds annoyed by their impatient holler.

I chew the hours; I chew the nights and days,
I rhyme my humble thoughts in every phrase.

# Gorgeous Eve

I haven't stopped to fall
Until my unexpected rise;
They called my fall spectacular,
They called my rise phenomenal.
I didn't have to climb the tallest wall
To see the Tower of Babel,
To see the tower of a heavy price,
To hear the godsent incoherent babble.

I am a doer; I am not a talker,
I am Adam; I am a high wire walker,
I pulled the winner-ace
From my long sleeve:
I noticed her attractive face,
Then picked her from the rabble
And kissed my gorgeous Eve.

I fell in love and melted like a snowflake,
It was a honeyed bite from the devil's cake:
She has become a vessel full of poison,
More vicious than a rattlesnake,
And yet, she was victorious in every fight,
Her splendor lingered in a parabolic flight
Above the virtuous but meek and frozen.

Today, my friends can see my tears,
My foes can hear my silent screams,
And yet, after so many years,
I love her, only in my morbid dreams.

# En Route

The sun is beaming
Not to be heard,
But to be seen.
The birds are singing
Not to be seen,
But to be heard.
Above the quiet blinded goddess Justice
That's even-handed and well-meaning,
But hesitates to use her rusty sword.

New problems fell on my tray,
I dreamed inside of my new suit,
A cab moved both of us along Broadway,
Continually entertaining everyone en route.

Within our ceaseless social upheaval,
Within our self-complacent times,
I dreamed about evenness of good and evil
Without punishments and crimes.

# Empty Dish

My so-called good decisions,
Were never smartly reasoned,
Were probably half-baked
And poorly seasoned.
The bad ones passed the tests of time,
They never turned around on a dime.

Whether created or discovered,
Things are just dated or devoured
By the forever merciless time.
We rearranged God's paradigm,
And only then lives had begun...
Nothing is new under the sun.

I combed through days,
No one was pure,
I combed across the nights,
No one was kind;
The justice was completely blind
And didn't see the bloody fights.

The nature birthed so many creatures:
The birds, the animals, and even fish;
This is why scientists and preachers
Still have in front of them an empty dish.

# Staircase

I keep my fingertips
On our life's irregular heartbeat,
And feverously lick my cracking lips,
Somebody grabbed my first row seat,
While the lifelong show is still going on,
And I don't want to hear the singing swan.

The poetry of science
Evokes the prose of silence,
And starts where the dice was thrown,
Right at the boundaries of the unknown.

Along the brave but careless
That fall from a frying pan into the fire,
Unless I choose the lesser of two evils
Between a six-headed Scylla
And vicious, murderous Charybdis,
Between two horns of a dilemma,
Between the heat of the abyss
And chill of a quagmire,
Between the condors and the eagles,
Between sweet candies and a lemon,
Between a rock and a hard place...

I chose the Heaven's staircase.

# Fallen Heroes

A moderator introduced the speakers
And briefly outlined their views;
A bunch of doubtful truth-seekers
Caressed their knowledge of the news
Injected into their religions,
And looked like empty-headed pigeons,
Who knew the answers for the questions
And had the guts to offer some suggestions.

The speakers cited the abyss and paradise,
But truth was not reflected in the sea of lies.

Futility of that debate
Was greatly elevated
And I rebuffed the bait,
That was too overrated.

It was quite obvious to me,
I knew a faster path to glee.

We cannot see our past in dusty mirrors,
Only the shiny ones reflect the real truth,
And show us the fallen heroes
Of our childhoods and youths.

# Before Swine

Some see beneath the shiny surface,
Some see beneath the crafty camouflage,
Some see the baffling future through the lace
Of the fat-chewers' verbal noneventful barrage.

I learned to effortlessly think,
At times, I even effortlessly rhyme and write;
Only my inborn gullibility is that weaker link
Which rarely lets me pick wrong from right.

I see the hammers of a societal neglect
Crashing the fragile crystal glasses
Lavishly filled with my poetic wine.
The future's grandeur is forever wrecked,
The opium of faith is given to the masses,
The pearls are squandered before swine.

## Ceaseless Fight

The end of war is peace,
The end of peace is war,
Life is a perpetual timepiece
I saw its dial many times before;
Life is a ceaseless fight
Amid the darkness and the light.

Today, it is a total darkness,
There is no dawn, no rising sun,
At night, there is no floating moon,
Even the falling star is sparkless;
That misery has gone
And not an hour too soon.

The same old show,
No intermissions,
The same old ebb and flow,
New actors, old additions
Demanding trick or treat.
The curtains never fall
Until the actors meet
St. Peter and St. Paul.

## So Long

I want your life to be like music,
That doesn't sink the boats,
That sounds like pacifying lullabies,
That is quite pleasingly amusing,
Without any cacophonic notes
Or other devils in disguise.

Life is a prison of conformity
It makes a perfect circle
Straight out of an edgy square;
Your freedom is a pure deformity
It is entirely anemic and infertile,
Like a lackluster love affair.

Eternity rotates me on its lathe:
I am the one, who didn't sell his soul,
Who didn't betray his faith
Like that infamous Dr. Faust;
I have a ripened, farfetched goal,
I want the moneychangers' oust.

I didn't live too long,
I even spent a day in the abyss;
I knew about right and wrong
Before the Judas kiss.

I will return one day; so long.

# Nonverbal

I want to be fully nonverbal,
I want to sow yet unknown seeds,
I want to be mysteriously herbal,
I want to paint and sink into the weeds.

They say the bell will toll for thee,
It is too apparent to ignore;
I asked my muse to set me free,
She caringly unlocked the door.

Life was and is a one-way street,
Just like a one-trick pony.
I waved a cab; I grabbed a seat:
"Hurry up and take me to my glee".

I traded my routinely wingless day
For the exciting, sparkling night:
We navigated through Broadway,
Wrapped in the quilt of my delight.

## Incurable

I am not a bird that likes his golden cage,
I am an actor that is starring on the stage.

The fourth dimension of our genders' distance
Produces thrashing of the sly love triangles
Into the boring squares of our existence
In which the geese are married to the ganders,
In spite of a never-ending justified resistance
To chronic, tireless, and incurable defenders.

Like all good things
Our marriage ended,
We threw away our wedding rings,
They quietly and gracefully landed.

No one will ever hear my laughter
In that evasive but a promised land,
Of course, if I will ever get in there.
No one will find me hereafter,
I'll be a drummer in a marching band,
And never leave my footprints in the air.

# Genuineness

Once the young twigs bend,
So grows the tree...
I use my every bloody cent
To buy my marihuana glee.

My life is worth the losing
Its ebbs and flows,
Its emperors without clothes;
My life is worth the boozing
With clowns and red noses
Through gains and losses;
My life is worth the choosing
Among my gives and takes
The genuineness of fakes.

I parented myself alone,
It was my happy start,
It is my happy end.
I let the others moan,
I know my sins by heart,
And I am ready to descend.

I've read the smaller print
And ran from truth in vain,
Just like a conniving pastor.
The end is a hasty sprint:
Today, I am moving faster,
I am encircling the drain.

It is my happy end,
I am ready to descend.

# Blindfolded Truth

I am not a boat without oars and sails,
I am not a train that chugs along the rails,
I am a want-to-know snooping boy,
Hiding under the pillow for his tooth fairy;

Years past; I ran across a vast periphery
Of our naïve creator's all forgiving ploy.

I lived in a glossy tower of lies,
I've read a never written verse,
I threw a never thrown dice,
I slept with the church's whores...

These games of my uneasy youth
In the pursuit of a vaguely known bliss
Were noticed by the blindfolded Truth,
Who said: "Don't even aim, you'll miss".

Life is a tragic comedy of ancient Greece:
We fight the wars, neglect a fragile peace,
But then the just and rigid Truth descends,
And none of us will reach the happy ends.

# Blunder

The low hanging apple
From the tree of knowledge
Was like a faithless chapel
Or rather a futile college
With useless preachers
Instead of caring teachers.

Today, I am walking toe to toe
With modern trends,
With enemies and friends
Who often stop to say hello
Without asking for amends.

Some break the speed of sound,
Some are forever in the weeds,
The others dig the ground,
Collecting the leftover seeds.

I only sow but hardly ever reap,
Don't judge me for the blunder,
I am just resting six feet under
And have a lot of time to weep.

But have no time to pay my debt,
Please, buy my verse on the internet.

# Pegasus

I satisfied my self-devouring desire
And read my gray-haired early verses:
Sometimes, they are intolerably dire,
Sometimes, they grace like highbred horses,
Sometimes, they are sweet and sentimental,
Sometimes, deliberately belligerent and vast,
Sometimes, pontificating and judgmental,
But always justly mirror my tormented past.

My soul already left my flesh
And hovers far above all those
Who hide their souls inside
To entertain their vanity and pride;
Who write their stillborn prose
And paid in rather weighty cash,
While I am devoted to my poetry.
I hold the reins of Pegasus and ride
Uphill, toward the wisdom tree...
Quite happy, yet deprived.

Each year, when spring arrives,
The world becomes a little younger,
For those who are deprived and strive
About six feet under.

# Sprint

My sketches create painterly equivalent
Of my occasionally lackluster lines.
I am no longer cautious and ambivalent,
Moving my words amid the warning signs.

I see the world; I take its pulse and write,
The scholars anxiously split hairs,
The critics never see the light,
While I discover bliss beyond despairs.

In life even a full-fledged comedy is tragic,
I hear our laughter through bitter tears.
Life is Charlie Chaplin's classic magic,
Still vivid after all these years.

The satin-finished face of our past
Expertly hides our wounds and scars,
But shows peace that couldn't last
And flaunts the perfect teeth of stars.

Our life is supposed to be a marathon,
But it is the fastest sprint before the end,
The final mile won't let you take the phone
And chew the fat with your beloved friend.

# Forgotten Art

Even the most flattering self-portraits
Will not let go premonition of the end
Even a critic-genius will not interpret
The meaning of the red line in the sand.

I saw ascending waterfalls of lights,
I saw descending sparkling fireworks,
I lived through the horrific wartime nights
When rockets pop like Champagne corks.

The nights of jarring color combinations,
The nights of black-and-white collisions
Entirely disregarded limits of my patience
And overstepped my damaged visions.

Long shadows whispered gentle lullabies,
I closed my weary eyes,
Then soared into the castle in the skies
And let the future cast the dice
Into a young and trembling dawn;
Life will not fail to go on
And cupids will not miss my heart.

In war love was a well forgotten art.

# Purest Well

My world is more mysterious inside,
Subconscious is my wisdom's purest well,
I went beneath my stumbled mind
And saw the room where my ideas dwell.

My eyes were reading out
A cryptic message on the wall
That looked like a hopeless shout,
Like a fragmented lingual waterfall
Under the arched colors of a rainbow,
Under its wonderfully creative glow.

Our existence is a test of courage,
Wisdom is tasted by our outrage,
Stupidity is just an empty storage,
A theatre with no actors on a stage.

Cicero said:"Vultus est index animi",
"The face reveals what's on the mind."
It's more trustworthy than alchemy,
Unless the person is completely blind.

Life is the Aladdin's hocus-pocus genie.

# Curiosity

My restless curiosity
Didn't allow me to settle down
And reinvent my life.
I could no longer stir and drive,
I gave away the shiny crown
Of my unleashed ferocity.

I lived among backbiters
And their unforgiven sins,
Among unpunished crimes
And quick "one-nighters"
In the highway inns…
I simply carved my rhymes.

I am sure my soul will not survive
My pompous burial today,
I lost my sparkling stubborn life
To those who steal and kill but pray.

# Requiem Descended

Responsibility is a load of power,
Accountability is just a crafty term,
It is a constant happy hour,
Paid to the lawyers by my firm.

You want to know
What is on my mind?
Look under my hood:
The winds still blow,
The blind still lead the blind,
The evil still defeats the good
In our godsent paradigm;
Meanwhile, I try to carve my rhyme.

The melody of requiem descended
As a sad homage to my life that ended
With countless losses and a few wins,
It couldn't swim and drowned in my sins.

## Discords

I slept along the glass-half-full sunsets,
I played along the glass-half-empty nights,
I used to place my thoughtless bets
The "kind" casinos let me win some fights,
But won the final merciless war.

At times, I think, therefore I am alive,
At times, I hide, therefore I will survive,
In spite of social predictable discords
Between the greedy hordes
Blinded by the red sunset,
The same as we first met.

We lost the pulse of our love's ebb and flow,
Our excitement ended,
The night descended,
I must go…

I bid farewell to every friend
And ask for their forgiveness;
I trust, the longest night will end
Wherever nearby Christmas.

# Everlasting Verses

I have a caustic vision of my critics,
Of those reviewing self-appointed nerds,
Of those cerebral paralytics
Who hate my fascination with the rhymes.
I mold and carve; I twist and turn my words,
Then let them cross the boundaries of times.

The Prince of light
Cast shades of doubt on my life;
The fallen angel cleared my sight:
"You have a view, equip yourself for strife,
You sin, correct yourself but don't confess,
Don't ever get familiar with remorse,
Exhibit only grace under your stress,
And life will get much better, never worse."

In vain, I asked:
"With what those four apocalyptic horses
Will substitute my everlasting verses?"
And heard: "Don't cry, they will be masked."

# Trivialities

Autumnal childhood's walks
Stubbornly lingered in my mind,
Just like the golden waterfalls
That played their sparkling tunes.
I bet, our forefathers weren't blind
When climbed the tallest walls
To argue with the passing moons.

I am stuffed with trivialities
Mixed with some real knowledge
Of up-to-the-minute scientific wings.
And yet, I drag the heavy baggage
Of clothes for emperors and kings,
And many other uneventful banalities.

Only the nasty and coldblooded snakes,
Only the messengers from underground,
Those carriers of our unending stress
Followed by the nervous breaks...
Beside the fallen angel heavens bound
Explain to us the virtues of finesse.

At times, I have no words
But paint or take quick photos
Invisible to anyone at first:
No footprints, just the sounds
That gift the human hounds
A chance to satisfy their thirst
For my poetic world without prose.

# Pink Slip

A huge unruly village,
Small hat, no cattle,
Small head, big mouth,
No plans before a battle;
It is a customary image
Of my beloved village,
Of my unruly South.

We picked this baton
From our forefathers,
We don't pursue an exit
From this unending maze,
We joined the hordes of others
Who want to see the end of days.

I can't accept what God created
And His submissive Saints affixed,
I try to change what has been fated,
I shake and stir what has been mixed.

I have no premonition of the failure,
I sent a pink slip to my sleepy Savior.

# Dog

My masterfully acting dog
Demanded yet another treat:
He staged his silent monologue,
He marched, I listened to the beat.

Under the jaded, sunless sky,
Beside the rules and trendy manners,
At times, under the flopping banners,
I lose my brittle sacred hope,
I realize, we both my dog and I
Pull the same side of a lifetime rope.

I used the twelve apostles of the jury
Against the mass's jealousy and fury,
I saw familiar trees in alien landscapes,
Of war and peace through lacy drapes.

Another hopeless night has gone,
Long live the rite of dawn.

## Sauternes

I am looking into my half-empty glass,
Half-fool with the scent of autumn grass,
A lump of blue cheese is lying on a side,
I have no words, I feel tongue-tied:
I am enjoying golden great sauternes...

I am in a paradise, I didn't earn.

# Abandoned Wisdom

I win my losses and lose my wins
While my abandoned wisdom slumbers;
I am familiar with a virtue and a vice,
My rescues don't exist without sins,
And yet, I dream of lucky numbers
And pitch my intuition with the dice.

I probably will live
In the sweet memories of hearts
Abruptly left behind,
And they will harshly sieve
The pearls of literary arts
So gently chiseled by my mind.

It was a premonition of my demise,
I felt it was my parting night,
I closed my eyes
And tried to fall asleep.
The angels heard my final breath
They didn't care and didn't weep,
They sent me a certificate of death
And calmly led me to the light
That was intolerably hot and red,
I was in the abyss, forever dead.

# Garments

Lives are the tiny fragments
Of the everlasting death,
That is invisible as garments
Of the pathetic walking emperor,
That is ethereal as a baby's breath,
Yet scary as the angry lion's roar.

It is like savagely sowed seeds
Among the brazen moneychangers
That poisoned all their deeds
And turned the losers to avengers.

Among us many have the watches,
The others have only time:
Some sip champagne on shady porches,
The others curse their lifelong climb.

# Loud Weepers

I walk the path away from the abyss
Over the so-called good intentions,
I simply want to rest in peace
And let the others get redemptions.

I haven't seen the real players
Among scorekeepers,
I haven't heard the heartfelt prayers
From the exuberantly loud weepers.

We are what we desire
And if the past was dire,
The future may be quite surprising,
After the nights the sun is rising...
I cannot be a mouthpiece for doom:
The hurricanes don't loom,
The sun caresses trees and fields,
I am expecting lavish yields.

I was His unexpected choice
I was sworn to secrecy by our Lord,
I clearly heard His voice
But won't reveal the sacred truth,
The primal word that started
Our childhood and youth,
The cornerstone of misery and glee,
The true location of the Wisdom Tree.

# Wedding Rings

I hardly know anything about women
Between eighteen and ninety;
They all demand the wedding rings,
I act as if I know what they mean
But wouldn't cross the final t
Until that awful lady sings.

I was manipulated my whole life,
Even my primal scream
A doctor forced out of me
And yet, I have a dream:
Never to do what I don't want
After I lost another futile strife;
Someone above has heard my plea
And let me choose my own font.

I hold my pleasures in crosshairs,
I wouldn't miss a single happy hour,
I am entirely spoiled by great wines
And by the weekends love affairs.

Only a daily so-called moral shower
Revives the common warning signs.

## Uninvited Tenants

Each actor is fairly represented on the stage,
The fiercest competition peacefully ended,
The mediocrity dismissed the real talents,
Only the last, only the final empty page
Remains untouched and not offended
By the upcoming uninvited tenants.

The density of a looming play
Was ultimately a plus,
Creating vibrancy rather than clutter;
It meant I have only one more day
To toss my foes under the bus
And pull my future from a gutter.

Even the passageways of powers
Lead all of us toward the walls
And we plant lifeless, wilted flowers
Over the shallow graves of our souls.

Only the tunnels lead us to the lights
And hopes that days will beat the nights.

## Being There

One cannot eat his honesty for lunch,
Nor can he use his dignity for dinner,
Only the fresh potato chips may crunch
And recognize a loser from a winner.

They say, no one can trust a skinny chef,
I went to church, into a local chapel
To prove that I am not blind or deaf,
To prove that I will be forever damned
If I don't prove that I descend from Adam
Who bit and chewed that famous apple.

The liturgy caressed the stained glass
Framed by the patient pointed arches,
The tides of music touched the shiny brass
Of icons with the Eden's fruitless branches;
The quiet ripples of a seductive tune
Were gracefully floating in the air
As if the polished silver of the moon
Enlightened us as a reward for being there.

## Unenviable Position

I am in the unenviable position,
I have to hear the referee, the judge,
I have to clean my tarnished pedigree,
I have to scrap the fudge.

And only then
A swan will sing its farewell song,
And only then
I will discover what went wrong.
And only then
I will receive the sentence,
Signed by the dozen of self-appointed gods,
Expecting my sincere repentance...

I didn't say a word, defying all the odds.

I tried but couldn't fool my fate;
I learned two truths, unfortunately, too late:
"Each man for himself!" and "Trust no one!"
From sunrise to sunset, from dusk to dawn.

# Rubicon

Eye-popping stories
Don't seek my humble verses,
They are those nervous horses
That left the barn
And gallop through my worries;
While I am left to spin my yarn.

I have no friends or enemies,
I am surrounded by frenemies,
And by the self-appointed earthly gods
Vigorously fishing with their rods
For paybacks, vanities and prides
For lives of greed without moral guides.

I have decided to look into myself,
And pulled the Bible from the shelf:
The Holy paradise was promised,
I learned to cherish my offenders,
I suffered from my so-called friends,
I wandered through the human forest
In the pursuit of happy ends,
I scrutinized the bushes and the trees,
I even hugged the ganders
And embraced the geese.

My search was fruitfully wise:
I sensed the self-indulging lies
Of those who marveled in the weeds
Above the quagmires of their deeds;

I saw the sugarcoated quilt of travesty
That numbed our integrity and honesty.

The Rubicon is crossed.
Sweet paradise is lost.

# Silly Props

Her eyes reflected an enduring fascination
With my prehistoric stories after I wiped their dust.
Meanwhile, I looked at her and hopelessly arrived
Into the most commanding sexual sensation,
Into a ceaseless, overwhelming lust.

I paid a lovely girl to strip,
She elegantly stripped,
And then I asked for more than that,
I pledged, she will be generously tipped;
Without a pointless chitchat
I liberally paid. She keenly flipped.

I know only one perversion,
It is a total lack of sex.
Everything else is just a choice,
Even if one deflowers a virgin,
Makes love to his abandoned ex,
Or uses the most unfamiliar sex toys.

Life is an assembly of silly props
Ridiculously stupid and annoying,
Only vibrating dildos are not the flops,
They are forever stiff and briskly toying.

# Heavy Drapes

I live behind the dusty windows
Shielded with the heavy drapes
From the unpredictable landscapes
Of our dreams as the singing goes.

I pull them up at nights,
I love the city neon lights,
I love their nightly beat,
It is my daily treat.

There is no armor against fate,
The commoners are equal to the kings,
Death grabs and leads us to the gate
Where even the sinless drop their wings.

The fools or the insanely brave,
No one is marching to the grave.
We enter our life and die alone,
The only days we claim as our own.

# Willing Necks

I saw a single trace left by the Third
And picked a feather of the Holy Bird;
The birds of feather flock together
Somewhere amid our sins and grace,
Under the regal Holy Trinity
Of our Father and His Son,
And the amazing ghostly Holy Spirit,
That charitably gave my soul
A password into infinity.
I hope the other two will hear it
And let me climb the Holy Totem Pole.

I knew my losses and my rare wins,
I walked into a haven of my failures,
Into a paradise of my unforgiven sins:
I raked the nasty and the nice
Far from my ears and eyes,
I didn't want to see or hear the preachers
And their prayers,
The lies and quarrels of those folks...

There were no willing necks
To wear the so-called moral yokes.

# Final Arbiter

I am not climbing like a mountain goat,
I hate the rocks left by the last Ice Age,
I saw a guy in a white-collared coat
And turned the closing page.

Death is the final arbiter
Of every human life,
No matter sweet or bitter;
We lose the lifelong strife.

New friendships and young wines
Are not reliable or lasting;
Yet every known law is usually bent,
I built me a wine cellar in the basement,
And treat my friends with daily lavish tasting,
We drink without reading any warning signs.

The stars in heavens are affixed,
The strangeness and elegance
Seem ordinary to the best of us,
Even a genius may be transfixed
By the invisible without evidence:
No doubts, nothing to discuss...

I failed to take my chances
And was severely punished at the end,
I didn't pay attention to nuances
And took an enemy for my best friend.

# Bluebird Sang

I twisted my ideas into the candy canes
To make them more attractive
For all the stubborn and hardheaded,
My needles were already threaded
And stitched together many brains
That still remained inactive.

The depth of expertise
Was quite illusory
In almost everyone I met;
I couldn't find any jewelry
In a provincial gazette,
I couldn't find any news
Under those fruitless trees...
Even a bluebird sang the blues.

I am not ashamed
Of my stigmatic mind,
I am not rich or famed,
I feel as if I am crucified,
But not resurrected.

Life was a busy stage,
I've read the script and acted,
But failed to read the final page.

# Sincere Bragging

I've never been a whisperer,
I wouldn't sneer behind your back,
My pistol doesn't have a silencer,
I am crystal clear like a loud soundtrack;

But I am very quiet in my pied-a-terre,
I try to hide my scrumptious love affair.

Bearing in mind my failures and forays,
My curiosity dissects the passing days
And leaves some low hanging fruits
To those who march in their dirty boots
Across my shaken and worn-out soul
And steal my sins to reach their goal.

I prize the evolution of my views,
And ramble in the puzzling venues
Amongst the fake ideas and illusions
Ignoring some half-baked conclusions.

I definitely have some strong opinions,
But I am not braindead opinionated,
I daily learn, my views are never dated.

At times, I even flaunt my brilliance.

# Ancient Lies

I cannot trust a preacher, who always beams,
I'd rather trust the one who seems
As if he is a clown with a lemon face,
As if he is a horse
That doesn't want to race,
As if he is a poet, who never wrote a verse,
And yet, even the longest thread,
Sooner or later sees its happy end.

I wish that preacher halts his ancient lies
Devoured as the manna from the skies
By those who still believe in paradise
And blindly trust this devil in disguise.

# Whores

I grew as a must-not-lose teenager:
Hard-hitting nights of a daily war,
My chancy life required a constant wager,
I always played, the others kept the score.

Then I received a letter from my friend,
I've read it all to its sarcastic end;
It said, "Your spouse cheats on us,
I thought she was an honest woman
We both can trust."

I wrote:" Please, take my wife,
I truly want to get away,
She is forever yours,
No animosity, no strife.
I'd rather dearly pay,
But for the real whores."

I showed grace in spite of stress
In the pursuit of a sparkling glee.
Here is my new address:
Davidson County, Tennessee.

# Depart

A tired summer called the undertakers,
An autumn flaunts its photogenic gold;
The bistros bring new cooks and bakers,
New seasons put old recipes on hold.

And then another winter has arrived,
No trumpets, just frozen minds deprived.
The breezes wrapped me in the ice,
I can no longer pick a virtue from a vice.

Worn-out winter left a few footprints,
No durable impact on anything,
No values to erase or cleanly rinse,
No bells to ring, no songs to sing.

A sunny spring moved into each heart,
And then a summer forced her to depart.
Nothing is new under the smirking sun,
Only four seasons calmly hit-and-run.

# Dusty Draperies

The faster run the modern times,
The shorter are the memories
Of struggles that are passing by.
I am encircled by the mimes,
They hang like dusty draperies
Designed to mute my final sigh.

No one composes requiems,
The bands don't play those tunes,
The generation of millenniums
Is not concerned with our wounds.

Our tears don't make them blind,
My death certificate is signed,
The highs of my amazing glee
Erased the footprints of my sorrows,
But saved the pages of my pedigree
Born in prehistoric human burrows.

# Frozen Gloom

Even the greatest parties end,
I said goodbye and kissed her hand,
The thrill was fading
As if it curbed its flow.
The blinding light is not enough
To sketch or paint our love,
It needs some shading,
It needs the sunset's afterglow,
A little darker but a happy ending.

I like the opulence and splendor of sunsets,
They so gently tremble in the quiet river;
I realize, we only dream, the gods deliver
Our gains and our debts.

The weary winter snow melts,
The yellow crocus bloom,
The birds begin to sing.
Farewell, the frozen gloom,
Strap your seatbelts
And rush to cheer the spring.

# Demonic Elf

Even a perky barbed wire,
Didn't protect me from the fall
Into a middleclass quagmire;
I failed to cover my mirages
With fierce linguistic acrobatics
Or with a quilt of colorful collages.

God knows where I have to be,
But doesn't know where I am,
I need to pray and take a knee...
But I am too busy making love,
And she is a tiger, not a lamb.
For me, love has its ebbs and flows,
For me, lovemaking is a poetic prose,
She thinks, I am just a loving dove.

With all the I's correctly dotted,
With all the t's precisely crossed,
Two lovers are securely knotted,
But I am absolutely lost.
I fly across the kingdom of nirvana
In the parabolic highs of marijuana.

Nobody comes to save me from myself;
I hope, I love a fairy, not a demonic elf.

# Egocentrics

Death is not a tragedy. A tragedy is life.
Death never ends. Life does.
I am worn out in a hunt for a falling knife,
And only death allows me to catch a buzz.

I didn't write this conflict-ridden epigram
To mock the Mathew's "Our Father" psalm.
There are no knives; just a few fallen angels.
I recognize among the lives of strangers
The wandering religious eccentrics,
The failed-to-get-attention egocentrics.

My word is just a tiny island in the oceans
Of mere indifference and banned emotions;
No one gifts courtesy to verified conclusions,
The masses drown in their own delusions.

# Discord

It is a Sunday mass, I hear my church's choir,
It sounds like the words descended from above.
Nevertheless, I want to be an object of desire,
I want to be a prisoner of love.

Don't ever ask, to be or not to be,
I am not your know-it-all guide,
I am not a coldblooded referee,
Of the rear-enders in your mind.

Life doesn't let me close with stitches
The gap between the old and young;
The silent void remains unfilled:
Life slams my daring pitches,
They fly above the battlefield,
The songs of victory remain unsung.

Sore point of debate,
An apple of discord,
A bone of contention...
It's all the same,
I learned to wait,
I simply pay a close attention,
Until somebody begs to strike a chord.

## Meridian

I sipped my scotch and puffed a thick cigar
Then fatefully crossed my fingers
Looking at the hesitantly falling star;
I am sure, my frail hope to win still lingers.

My glee hides in tomorrows,
I cannot see or hear that far.
I merely collect my sorrows
And meet my buddies in the bar.

I can no longer hear my own voice,
I need to be somebody else;
My loneliness has made its choice:
I am a new meridian and date the parallels.

# Utopian Boneyard

The Son has lost his earthy strife
And got another chance above the ground.
But we will never see the promised better life,
But we will never get into the second round.

I circled the Place de la Concorde,
I cut my teeth in search of the Elysian Fields,
There is a place for my nostalgic wreath
On the forgotten graves of gods and heroes,
Whose deeds reflected in the crooked mirrors.

My memories lazily float along the Seine River,
Wrapped in a heavy morning fog.
I sail my old, dilapidated boat
In the pursuit of yesterdays,
Just like a hungry hound dog
I fetch the hidden exit from the maze.

At last, I raked the bits of yesteryears
Into a monument for enemies and peers.
These days, I am their loyal witty guard,
I whistle Dixie past that utopian boneyard.

It is the place where rubber meets the road,
I am paying for their sins I've never owed.

# Left Behind

I gravitate toward the depth of love,
To see my raw emotions from above
And clarify my soul and mind,
I want to know what I had left behind.

Is it a boring prose? Is it a classic rhyme?
Is it a critical discourse
Against the cruel hegemonic paradigm?
For better or for worse,
It is a punishment without a crime,
It is the pale apocalyptic horse.

# Divine Comedy

I know those who clutch the key
Into the never-ending glee,
I am terrified of dumb good-doers,
They act far outside their thinking,
Their efforts quickly fill the sewers,
While we are thankfully blinking.

Columbus, Vikings, and Magellan,
Vespucci and Vasco De Gamma
Mistook our planet for a melon
And rolled the Dante Divine comedy
Into the Devil's drama.

They went beyond the old horizons,
They crisscrossed our ragged globe
Regardless of many dos and don'ts,
They found the new world and hope.

They changed the Pillars of Gibraltar
Into the stormy strait of Heracles,
We like our traveling hereafter,
Meanwhile, they RIP in Père Lachaise.

# Deceit

I stood in front of a sunlit wall:
A soothing sense of free-for-all
Established a sentimental unity
Among exposure and immunity,
Among my loyal, bosom friends
And convoluted modern trends.

I wondered who created our world,
The Big Bang or the primal word;
Then stretched the Milky Way
And parted predators from prey.

I wondered whether the spirits' jury
That slowly reestablished sanity,
Will curb the other climbing fury
The self-inflicted pride and vanity.

I wondered why I bought a ticket,
And took a next-to-a-window seat,
My train has never left the station,
And I escaped a thoughtful deceit
Explaining evolution and creation.

## Boneless

My future pulled a rabbit from its hat:
Dark, numb, hostile, and feisty;
Life cloned a hanging upside-down bat:
Aggressive, ugly, but cold as an ice-tea.

I can no longer tolerate stupidity,
I choose a perpetual aloneness,
But not a crowded infinity,
Where even the graves of our souls
Are flowerless and boneless...
Perhaps they all achieved their goals.

Infinity is not a gift,
It is an ascending drift:
The dead deserve to rest in peace and silence,
And yet, we hear the roar of human violence,
And ask the one who gave us life:
Can you create just peace without strife?

## Solitary Dialogue

My solitary dialogue with empty pages
Descends into the uninspiring truce:
"Let us agree to disagree."
And yet, I try to save the golden goose,
But lose emotional highways
Between my verses with my plays.

I write anew and set my verses free,
Then lure them back and lock their cages.
They are my gifted actors,
The world is full of empty stages.

# Worthwhile

Sometimes, I lose my way
And get into the weeds,
But still, under the Milky Way,
Reflected in my wisdom beads.

I never worked a day in life,
I drank my glee from firehoses,
Life was a thorny bed of roses,
But never a disgusting wife.

My thoughts enjoy a short shelf live,
Each one is understood and thrives,
As if I sowed the semen and reaped the birth,
As if I earned to leap into a paradise on Earth.

In spite of those who hold the keys
From the evasive gates upstairs,
In spite of a life in their crosshairs,
I chose my own expertise:
I promised to a friend
To walk an extra mile,
And reach the happy end
That makes our lives worthwhile.

# Disillusions

I truly hoped to curb my anger
And see a better side of everyone,
To see a bug in every amber
As evidence of an ancient hit-and-run.

I thought I breathed above the fray,
I dreamed about equality and peace,
But life has chosen its own way
And I lost the forest for the trees.

I saw the same ole' pushers
Of ignorance and lies
Still hiding in the bushes,
And waiting for the sun to rise.

Those horrors gather on my plate,
I see them through a lens of fear,
They wouldn't disappear,
I could no longer wait;
I pulled the trigger of my gun,
My disillusions learned to run.

# Clown

Life-hurricane swirls by,
My guiding beacon looks
As if it might leap off the cliff
And hover with the birds
Above the dolphin herds.

I try to guess not when but if
I'll see another dawn or die.

I didn't step up to the plate,
I chose to watch and wait...

It seems, those days have gone,
When I was carelessly insane,
Today, I am blinded by a dawn
Today, I am walking with a cane.

I would invent a better paradigm,
If I could make a U-turn and go back,
Just once upon a time,
And patch each worthy crack...

In vain, I jam my squares into the circles,
Regrettably, I miserably fail,
And look like a stupid clown in a circus
Or rather a wrecked mast without a sail.

# Final Battlefield

I crawled across my final battlefield of war,
I twisted like a snake between my fallen brothers;
My hungry, skinny body in a bloody camouflage,
Was smart and brave but caught in that barrage.

It happens at the end of wars:
I stood on my all fours
And roared as the angry lion
Who knows that he survived,
But his belief in reason died.

These days I mumble, "C'est la guerre".
We live our lives, but wars are never fair.

A life with many doubts
Beats death without them;
I know all the ins and outs,
In life I am a mighty lion,
In death I am a lamb.

## Flying Cranes

The wedge-shaped blocks
Stop in their tracks
My victories and losses;
The wedge-shaped flocks
Of the southbound flying cranes
Remind me of the flowing knifes
Above the wedge-shaped trees
That let an early morning breeze
Chill out and appease
Our troubled lives.

We read it in old books
With tattered pages:
Our trees and hedges
Prefer the wider edges
To hide our quiet nooks.

# Rekindled

The others see my greed
That moves the lever;
I wish the angels plead
To help my new endeavor.
I hold both ends of life's equation,
All boats are lifted by a single tide,
I will make my mind up on this occasion.

I am marching toe-to-toe
With the trendsetters of this time,
They keep my feet close to the fire,
But I rekindled my desire:
I always craved to be a stone's throw
From secrets of the godsent paradigm.

I strip-searched every corner of my life,
But didn't find roots of our endless strife;
My girlfriend thinks I am a saint,
She is confused, a saint I ain't.

## Addicted

If a few nights in Reno
Have taught me anything,
It's that being smart is not enough.
No one can win in the casino
Unless you have two angel' wings
And learn to camouflage your bluff.

The game of poker
Is like a castle in the sky,
They treat you as a futile joker,
Unless you learn to eat and have a pie,
Then you may afford a tip to your croupier,
Instead of just a stingy "Bonsoir, Monsieur."

I studied all of the above,
I am smart; I am lucky, and quite gifted.
But finally, push came to shove,
I moved to Reno to sleep under the bridge,
And wash the dirty dishes. I am addicted.

# Freezing Waterfall

I never climbed the stairs to truth,
Life was a constant fight,
I battled nail and tooth
To find my birthright.

I wore my wounds and every scar
As the most valued war awards,
She kissed them while we were hugging in a car,
Evading curiosity of similarly cuddling hordes.

Reality was eager to arrive,
Just like a freezing waterfall.
I waited in the fertile fields,
Expecting overwhelming yields,
But life I lived has never been a lavish friend,
Even my birthright doesn't have the happy end.

# Already Psychedelic

My face absorbed repulsion and confusions
After I pierced the crowd with my eyes,
I could forgive myself for some delusions,
But not for my trust in the world's demise.

I still possess a seemingly unlimited desire
To change the present run-down paradigm
Then from a single spark to start a fire
And morph the night into a bright daytime.

I picked the fruit of wisdom in my garden,
Then went to church to see my padre.
After my confession and remorse,
I grabbed from him a pardon,
And wrote this rustic verse.

All of a sudden, I became angelic,
Even the saints befriended me;
I floated on my pair of wings,
The rainbows were already psychedelic,
Just like a multicolored tempting glee
Of vivid fables and never-ending springs.

# Damoclean Sword

The moon slips lower in the skies,
The stars unmanly blink goodbyes,
The hills rise high to fight the sleepy giant,
Forever bored to death but self-reliant,
The valleys dig their trenches deeper
To hide the creeks from the hostile sleeper.

Everyone gets ready for a war,
But looks for a bone of contention
To figure out what's worth fighting for.
I've seen this film so many times before,
This time I pay close attention.

My view is based on a broken-window's logic,
I sense the same old story of aggression
I don't anticipate any solution, any magic,
But I foresee the bloodshed, deficits and rations.

The moment they created the apple-of-discord,
They hung above us their Damoclean sword.

# Sunday Schools

False advertisement is a common crime.
The gods and saints created a self-serving paradigm,
In which we live and want to enter the abyss or bliss,
Are forced to play the chancy game of hit-or-miss,
But there is no room in space for trillions of souls,
That haven't read the Dead Sea Scrolls.

Another day approached its own sunset,
I craved to throw something on my tooth,
I bought a chunk of meat, a French baguette,
And a jug of brandy, the real fountain of youth
That ironed my worn-out face:
No wrinkles, that looked like my senses lace,
No victories over the deadly ills,
No failures and no thrills.

Since rather a syrupy nirvana of my Sunday schools,
I try to stay away from the ship of fools...

# Thoughts

I don't cannibalize my thoughts,
I use them in a single verse
And let them go.
They find their own pots
And vigorously grow
To be sold for money just like whores.

My thoughts are like exciting flowers
In my so-called artistic basket,
I use them as the compelling powers
To heal some psychological disorders;
The problems burst out of their casket
And run beyond the reason's borders
To find someone who can freely breathe,
And gift a shotgun drawn from a sheath.

## Broken Lanterns

Not every dog had fleas,
Not every cat was gray at night,
Not every naked tree performed striptease,
Not every tunnel would show at its end the light...

I am sure, exceptions justify the rules
Acknowledged by the wise and fools;
I am surrounded with the signs "past tense",
To see tomorrows, I look beyond the fence.

A tale of love between a raven and a cardinal,
Kept my adolescent listeners in stitches,
I walked them through the everlasting carnival,
Avoiding sinister quagmires and muddy ditches.

I am following our Mother Nature's chapter,
I am finishing the final chapter
Of my self-serving memoirs.
As if I am drinking wine from famous terroirs.

The stars are blinking like broken lanterns,
I am raking heavens in the pursuit of phantoms.

# Heaven Bound

When someone has been shot or drowned
In yet another bloody strife,
The gods don't know if he is heaven bound,
And wouldn't even call his wife.
She hopes he is a prisoner of war,
She waits. She never locks the door.

So many years passed by,
The kids have grown,
Left home and waved goodbye,
That day her hopes away have flown.

Nobody takes the blame,
The world remains the same,
Her sons will fight another war...
At last, she shut the door.

# Birthday Suit

The primal word created my imagination,
I walked across that famous Eden's garden,
I rested in the shades of both amazing trees
Of everlasting life and carnal knowledge,
Intrigued by the interwoven good and evil.
I didn't need to study in a private college,
To grasp, it was the first in history striptease.
Adam and Eve were begging for a pardon
In presence of the unescapable upheaval
After the great theatricals of their creation.

I didn't pick that low hanging fruit,
I wore Armani, not a birthday suit.

There is always the beginning and the end,
Even infinity is somewhat a fragile hope
Of those who have the upper hand,
But hanging on the rope
Between a life and the devouring black hole,
Between lovemaking and the birth control.

# History Apologizes

My rhyme runs like a thread
Through every verse I tailor,
From bits and cuts I know,
From hunger 'till a daily bread,
From a creator 'till a jailer,
From fires 'till the embers glow.

I might have known in my youth
A few conniving friends.
They never parted lies and truths,
They fed me with the happy ends.

I seldom run my eyes
Across the morning paper,
I watch TV and hear the news,
And use those that adjust my views.

I comb the global multilingual crowds:
The feisty eagles and the loving doves.
The killers and the healers.
I am ready to unfurl the shrouds
Of callous wheeler-dealers,
Corrupting our loyalties and loves.

The sun still rises
Yet nothing changes
Under its caring beams.
Only the history apologizes,
Because it still rewrites and rearranges
Our lies, betrayals and shameful dreams.

# Backbiting Dragnet

I am not bloodthirsty, I was drafted,
I simply went into the grinder
Which the warmongers crafted...
Allow me a minuscule reminder:
Only the fallen saw the end of war;
I luckily escaped the final score.

So many moons have passed,
I am back in Vietnam at last:
As in the tortured past,
I walk along the fields of rice and grain,
As in the bloody past,
I am pierced by the darts of endless rain;
The sun surrounded to overcast;
I walk and whisper: I miss my brothers,
I don't miss the pain.
Vietnam is not a magnet,
It is a backbiting dragnet
That rakes the ugly, bad and good,
And lets us pick under our own hood.

# The Riddles of The Sphinx

The memory-bell rings,
Only its echo narrows,
We cracked
The riddles of the sphinx,
We tracked
The guards of pharaohs,
Shielding the god-kings
Against the flying arrows.

They died, but brought us
"Egypt for the dummies",
The pyramids, the lotus
And miserable mummies
As valuable backbones
Of brilliant civilizations,
The magic cornerstones
Of restless newer nations.

We never mourn
Those ancient kings
To whom we owed,
We only mourn
Those morbid kings
To whom we loaned.

## Weaker Link

I even tasted courage in a brutal war,
But wisdom locked from me its door:
Erratically, I am sober or use a shrink,
But then I gratefully sink into my drink.

I used a straw to sip my mother's milk,
I tried to rearrange my drinking habits,
My DNA refused to fix its weaker link,
My hat is empty; no more rabbits.

# Younger Swine

One of the fallen angels
Entered through my window,
I poured two glasses of Champagne
And welcomed a distinguished guest
Into my much-loved temporary limbo,
But left this station on a morning train.

I am no longer nodding to the past,
I want tomorrows of my own design,
Regrettably, my strange ideas didn't last,
I still cast pearls but to a younger swine.

That angel left his image in my mirror,
A handsome face of a fearless hero;
Veronica wiped a stoic face of Jesus
With her tattered veil,
Unfortunately, to no avail:
The image of a Christ did not survive
A promised peace failed to arrive.

# Epilogue

I couldn't cross the threshold of a loud fame,
I failed; I stumbled on my unassuming verses;
I hope, my poetry survives the merciless flame
That will be brought by four apocalyptic horses.

# Acknowledgments

I am grateful to Judith Broadbent, my discerning editor,
for her highly cultivated sensibilities and generosity offered
to me.
For her unyielding yet wise editing,
Which allows me enough room to exercise my whims.

To Anna Dikalova for her kind ideas
And a firm belief in my success.

To a great artist, Mary Anne Capeci,
Who graciously allos me to use
Her painting for the cover of this book.

To all my friends for their continuous
And gently expressed motivations.

Thank you all, PZ

Printed in the United States
by Baker & Taylor Publisher Services